ACTIVITIES

Art and Design Projects

AGES 5-11

LORI VANKIRK SCHUE

AUTHOR
Lori VanKirk Schue

CURRICULUM ADVISER
Alison Milford

SENIOR COMMISSIONING EDITOR
Juliet Gladston

ASSISTANT EDITOR
Tracy Kewley

DESIGNER
Geraldine Reidy

ILLUSTRATOR
Gary Shipman

PUBLISHED BY
Scholastic Ltd,
Villiers House,
Clarendon Avenue,
Leamington Spa,
CV32 5PR
www.scholastic.co.uk

This edition is published by arrangement with
Evan-Moor Corporation, USA. Text © 2004
Evan Moor Corporation

© 2005 Scholastic Ltd

Designed using Adobe Indesign

Printed and bound by Tien Wah Press Ltd,
Singapore.

1234567689   5678901234

British Cataloguing-in-Publication Data

A catalogue record from this book is
available from the British Library.

ISBN 0-439-96526-8
ISBN 978-0-439-96526-2

Extracts from Programmes of Study from
The National Curriculum reproduced under
the terms of HMSO Guidance Note 8.
© Qualifications and Curriculum Authority.

The rights of Lori VanKirk Schue to be
identified as the Author of this work has
been asserted by her in accordance with
the Copyright, Designs and Patents Act
1998.

CONTENTS

Introduction

This book offers a wide range of projects developed to introduce children to a variety of art media and techniques. The book is divided into six chapters, each covering a different art and craft medium. Each chapter contains a variety of projects that enable children to investigate the medium in depth.

The book can be used in several ways:

- for activities and skills on a specific art medium such as weaving.
- for activities and skills based on a specific art technique such as printing.
- as a dip-in resource to find an interesting art activity for a specific occasion or lesson.

Some of the chapters contain additional information on their art subject. For example, the chapter on clay gives detailed tips on the handling and use of clay. This information can be for your own use or incorporated into an art lesson.

We recommend that you do each project ahead of time in order to anticipate any special assistance that may be needed.

After a project is completed, discuss the artwork. Allow the children to critique their own works by finding something they like and something they don't like about the finished product.

At the back of the book there is a glossary of words and terms used in the book. The glossary can be used as a reference for teachers and to re-inforce children's art vocabulary while they are working on an art topic.

Using the project pages

Each project is broken down into the areas outlined below:

Age range

This section highlights the recommended age range. Most of the projects can be adapted for less able or more able children.

Curriculum links

This section gives direct links to the relevant Government documents such as the National Curriculum and the QCA Schemes of Work. These links can help you with the planning and assessment of future activities.

Vocabulary

These are words used as part of the project. All the terms can be found in the glossary at the back of the book.

Materials

In this section, you will find a concise list of resources needed for each project. Aim to get the resources ready and set out before the project is started.

Project notes

This a bulleted list of additional information that will help to ensure that the project is a success.

Let's talk about it

This section gives examples of questions that can be used to encourage children to discuss the art techniques and ideas used in each project.

Steps to follow

This section gives concise step-by-step instructions on how to carry out the art activity. It is accompanied by detailed diagrams and illustrations.

Information box

Some of the projects have additional information boxes that provide tips and explain special techniques.

Display

- Creating pieces of art is a rewarding experience and children's work should be displayed whenever possible. Children have a sense of achievement when they see their finished work on display. It encourages them to discuss, compare and appreciate each other's individual creativity and perspective.

- Work can be displayed on both flat walls or moveable boards.

- Window ledges, counters, table tops and bookcases make excellent display areas for three-dimensional pieces.

- Large pieces such as papier-mâché animals or brooms can be displayed on a floor area. Mark out the area with masking tape or cloth. Set up blocks or stools to serve as stands for the art piece.

- Don't forget to label each piece with its title, the medium used, the artist's name and the date created.

Painting

From an early age, most children love to paint pictures as a creative activity. As they grow older, they discover that painting, as a medium, can cover a wide range of processes, techniques, styles, materials and tools.

The projects in this chapter allow children to learn and gain experience in a wide range of painting techniques and styles. They develop skills in painting still life using vegetable prints and textured paint, learn and use watercolours, and paint abstracts using different types of paint. The projects also allow the children to explore art styles such as Cubism and the delicate oriental brushstrokes of Wang Yani.

All the projects encourage children to experiment with the use of colour, texture, form, line and pattern. A colour wheel at the end of the chapter clearly explains the use of colour mixing and tones.

There are many opportunities to paint within the learning environment. As children experience the different forms of painting, they can start to establish skills and knowledge that will enhance their own creativity.

Contents

Crazy animals

Age range: 5–11 years

Learn to use familiar shapes and watercolour paints to create an abstract animal.

Vocabulary

abstract

painting

priming

Materials

- watercolour set with brush
- 23 x 30.5 cm or 30.5 x 46 cm white art paper
- cup for water
- paper towels
- black crayon

Project notes

- This easy project teaches children how to work with watercolours. Watercolour is different from tempera paint because it is coloured water instead of opaque paint. Children who have used tempera paint know they can easily correct a mistake by simply letting the paint dry and painting over it. This is not the case with watercolour. It is also important to teach children how to get the paint set ready to use by priming it to soften the pigment (see page 7).

Let's talk about it

- What is abstract painting?
- How is watercolour different from tempera paint?
- What are the different shapes we can use to create interesting animals?

National Curriculum: Art & design
KS1: 1a, 1b, 2a, 2b, 2c, 4a, 4b, 5b, 5c
KS2: 1a, 1b, 2a, 2b, 2c, 4a, 4b, 5b, 5c
QCA Schemes of Work: Art & design
Unit 1B – Investigating materials
Unit 3B – Investigating pattern
Scottish 5–14 Guidelines: Art & design
Using materials, techniques, skills and media:
Using media; Using visual elements
Expressing feelings, ideas, thoughts and solutions:
Creating and designing; Communicating

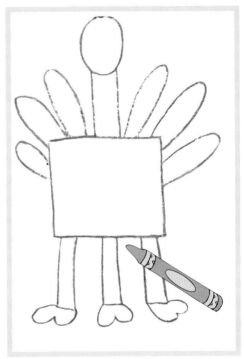

Step 2

Steps to follow

1 As a class, brainstorm and list different shapes. Ask the children to name animals. Discuss the shapes that might be used to create them. A horse, for example, might be made from an oval body and head, rectangular neck and legs, and triangular hooves and ears. Draw some examples on the board.

2 Draw the outline of the animal with black crayon on the art paper, then paint the animal with primed watercolours.

3 Let each child choose an animal and experiment with several designs on a sheet of scrap paper. They can then paint their favourite design on the art paper. Encourage them to use many different shapes and colours.

4 Set the paintings aside to dry.

Step 2

How to prime a watercolour set

Before using the watercolours, put a few drops of water on each colour to soften the paints. The water will loosen the pigment and give a richer colour.

Colour blocks

Create a painting using geometric shapes and complementary colours.

Vocabulary

complementary colours

Cubism

geometric design

Materials

- 30.5 x 46 cm white paper
- tempera paint
  (various colours in cups)
- brushes
- broad-tip black marker
- pencil
- ruler or straight edge

Project notes

- This technique was originally developed by several artists in Paris in the early 1900s. They were called Cubists because of their frequent use of geometric motifs. Talk about Cubism and show examples of paintings by Piet Mondrian. Discuss how Mondrian liked to paint with straight lines and right angles.

- Discuss complementary colours and why they are effective in this sort of painting.

- Arrange the children into groups so that they can work with each other and share supplies.

Let's talk about it

- Does your painting seem restful or busy?
- How does using black marker clarify the artwork?

National Curriculum: Art & design
KS1: 1b, 2a, 2b, 2c, 4a, 4b, 4c, 5b, 5c
KS2: 1b, 2a, 2b, 2c, 4a, 4b, 4c, 5b, 5c
QCA Schemes of Work: Art & design
Unit 1B – Investigating materials
Unit 3B – Investigating pattern
Scottish 5–14 Guidelines: Art & design
Using materials, techniques, skills and media:
Using media; Using visual elements
Expressing feelings, ideas, thoughts
and solutions: Creating and designing;
Communicating

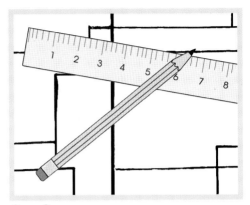

Step 2

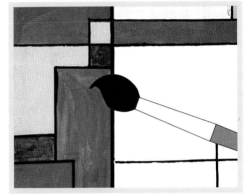

Step 3

Steps to follow

1 Decide whether to work on the horizontal or vertical orientation of the paper (landscape or portrait).

2 Develop the design by sketching with a pencil, using a ruler or straight edge. Try not to divide the design directly in half on the paper. Add interest by grouping smaller shapes in one area and larger ones around them.

3 Paint each section of the design using complementary colours. Encourage the children to leave some white space to keep the painting bright and airy.

4 When the painting is completely dry, the children may use a black marker and ruler to redraw the original pencil lines.

Complementary colours

Complementary colours are pairs of colours that are opposite each other on the colour wheel. Children need to experiment with these colours to understand that they are powerful when used together. Complementary colours may appear to vibrate when placed side by side in a painting. The three pairs of complementary colours are:

red – green

blue – orange

yellow – violet

Note: Pages 22 and 23 contain an explanation of the colour wheel and a photocopiable colour wheel.

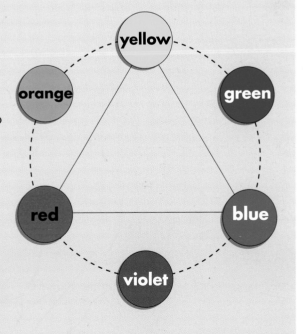

Stained-glass windows

Age range: 5–11 years

Create a painting that looks like a stained-glass window by using fingerpaint and tissue paper.

Vocabulary

medium

technique

transparent

Materials

- white tissue paper (any size)
- tempera paints
- liquid starch
- black marker
- card (for frame)
- bowls

Project notes

- This simple project gives children experience of finger painting on a more sophisticated level.

- Show some samples of stained-glass windows. Point out the coloured glass and the lead that separates each colour and helps to hold the glass together. Discuss the wonder of the transparent effect when the glass is held up to the light.

- Set up a work area and ask the children to wear smocks. Choose an area for drying paintings before you start. Work with one small group at a time.

Let's talk about it

- What medium was used in this painting?
- Why use fingers instead of brushes in this project?
- What gives this painting a transparent look?

National Curriculum: Art & design
KS1: 2a, 2b, 2c, 4a, 4b, 5b, 5c
KS2: 2a, 2b, 2c, 4a, 4b, 5b, 5c
QCA Schemes of Work: Art & design
Unit 1B – Investigating materials
Unit 3B – Investigating pattern
Scottish 5–14 Guidelines: Art & design
Using materials, techniques, skills and media:
Using media; Using visual elements
Expressing feelings, ideas, thoughts
and solutions: Creating and designing;
Communicating

Step 2

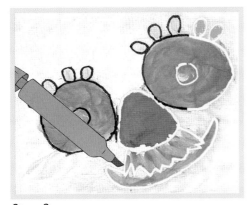

Step 3

Step 4

Steps to follow

1 Lay the tissue paper flat on the table. Decide what to paint.

2 Using fingers and the paints, create a picture using lots of different colours.

3 Set the painting aside to dry. When the painting is completely dry, trace around every shape with a black marker to resemble the lead in a real stained-glass window.

4 Create a card frame for the painting. Hang the children's paintings in a window and enjoy the transparent effect.

How to mix the finger paint

Use half a cup (120 ml) of tempera to quarter of a cup (60 ml) of starch. Mix a bowl of colour for every colour on the colour wheel.

How to frame a transparent picture

Cut two pieces of card 10 cm wider and longer than the painted image. Cut out the centre of one piece, leaving a 5 cm border around the outside. Paste the tissue paper painting between the paper pieces to create a frame effect.

Vegetable bouquet

Age range: 5–11 years

Watercolour techniques combine with tempera vegetable prints to create a vibrant still life.

Vocabulary

background   foreground

printing   painting

technique

Materials

- watercolour set with brush
- cup for water
- white art paper
- salt
- celery stalk (cut close to the bottom)
- sweet pepper (sliced across to form flower shape)
- onion (sliced across to show texture)
- flat dishes for tempera paint
- tempera paint

Project notes

- This project uses the watercolour techniques of gradated wash, wet on wet, wet on dry, and using salt to add texture. Printing with tempera paint is combined with the watercolour techniques. Practise watercolour and printing techniques before starting the project.

- Set up all of the materials before starting. To prevent accidents, the children should remain seated while

Let's talk about it

- What is a still life?
- How can painting and printing be used in the same piece of artwork?
- How is watercolour different from tempera paint?

National Curriculum: Art & design
KS1: 1a, 2a, 2b, 2c, 4a, 4b, 5b, 5c
KS2: 1a, 2a, 2b, 2c, 4a, 4b, 5b, 5c
QCA Schemes of Work: Art & design
Unit 2B – Mother Nature, designer
Unit 3B – Investigating pattern
Unit 5A – Objects and meanings
Scottish 5-14 Guidelines: Art & design
Using materials, techniques, skills and media:
Investigating visually and recording; Using media;
Using visual elements
Expressing feelings, ideas, thoughts and solutions:
Creating and designing; Communicating

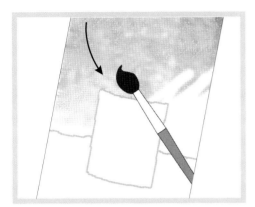

Step 2

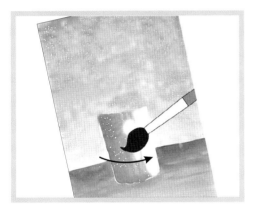

Step 4

Step 6

Steps to follow

1 Turn your paper to the vertical position. After priming the watercolour set, draw a simple shape for a vase and a table line behind the vase.

2 Brush clean water from the top of the paper to the table line, leaving the vase area dry. Drop a few brushloads of different colours onto the water (wet on wet technique). Colours will be fuzzy and will create a background for the flowers.

3 While the paint is wet, sprinkle salt in different areas to add texture. Let the painting dry thoroughly before removing the excess salt.

4 Brush clean water on the vase area. Add paint on the left-hand side. Using vertical strokes, continue to paint water on the rest of the vase to create a gradated wash. The vase should be dark on the left-hand side and light on the right-hand side.

5 Paint the table area with another colour (wet on dry technique). Let the paint dry.

6 Pour several bright colours of tempera paint into flat plates or trays. Dip the end of the celery into the paint and print several 'flowers'. Continue the same process with the other vegetables to create a 'bouquet.'

7 Using watercolour, add green stems and leaves.

Fish pond

Age range: 5–11 years

Develop a water scene by combining watercolour with printing.

Vocabulary

impression

pigment

technique

Materials

- 23 x 30.5 cm or 30.5 x 46 cm watercolour paper
- watercolour set
- brushes (large and small)
- cling film (enough to cover the paper generously)
- black tempera paint
- small fresh fish
- newspapers or paper towels
- sponge for clean-up
- bucket of water

Project notes

- Set up a station for printing and let a few children print at a time.
- Wash the fish in a bucket of water and then dry them between each print so that the texture of the fins and scales will show.

Let's talk about it

- What technique gave the impression of moving water?
- What do the fish prints add to this painting?
- Does the placement of the fish suggest movement?

National Curriculum: Art & design
KS1: 1a, 2a, 2b, 2c, 4a, 4b, 5b, 5c
KS2: 1a, 2a, 2b, 2c, 4a, 4b, 5b, 5c
QCA Schemes of Work: Art & design
Unit 1B – Investigating materials
Unit 3B – Investigating pattern
Unit 4A – Viewpoints
Scottish 5–14 Guidelines: Art & design
Using materials, techniques, skills and media:
Investigating visually and recording; Using media;
Using visual elements
Expressing feelings, ideas, thoughts and solutions:
Creating and designing; Communicating

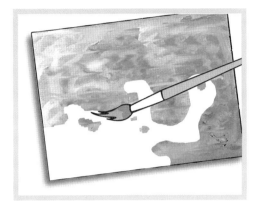

Step 2

Step 3

Step 6

Steps to follow

1 Wet the watercolour paper generously with water.

2 Prime the watercolour set. Then drop large brushloads of blue and green pigment onto the paper until it is covered.

3 Lay the cling film over the wet, painted paper. Let any wrinkles and bumps remain. DO NOT smooth the film. Tap the cling film down gently and let the paint dry completely.

4 Remove the cling film.

5 Dry the fish with paper towels and paint one side with black tempera paint.

6 Print the fish by placing the painted side of the fish onto the painted paper and pressing with newspaper or paper towels. Add as many fish prints as needed to complete the design.

Dancing monkeys

Age range: 7–11 years

This project imitates the art of Wang Yani and the Oriental style of painting using a limited palette.

Vocabulary

limited palette

Materials

- watercolour set
- thick and thin brushes
- 15 x 46 cm pieces of paper – two per child
- cups for water
- paper towels

Project notes

- Prime only the red and black watercolours. Make the watercolour very 'soupy'.
- Children need to practise with large and small brushes. Thick brushstrokes are best for the monkeys' arms and legs, and thin strokes for fingers, toes, and details.

Share the Art of Wang Yani

Introduce the artist Wang Yani by showing prints of her work. Point out that she uses only simple brushstrokes and creates movement in her pictures by the way she paints the elbows and knees of her subjects.

Let's talk about it

- Why are Chinese-style paintings so different from European artwork?
- Do all paintings tell a story?
- What mood do the Chinese paintings convey?

National Curriculum: Art & design
KS1: 2a, 2b, 2c, 4a, 4b, 4c, 5b, 5c
KS2: 2a, 2b, 2c, 4a, 4b, 4c, 5b, 5c
QCA Schemes of Work: Art & design
Unit 1B – Investigating materials
Unit 6A – People in action
Scottish 5–14 Guidelines: Art & design
Using materials, techniques, skills and media:
Using media; Using visual elements
Expressing feelings, ideas, thoughts
and solutions: Creating and designing;
Communicating

Step 2

Step 3

Step 4

Steps to follow

1 Demonstrate how to use simple brushstrokes to create monkey body parts such as those shown on page 16. Use both thick and thin brushes. You might gather children around you or paint on the overhead projector.

2 Allow the children to use a sheet of paper to practise strokes. Encourage them to try many different techniques for creating separate monkey body parts. They should use only black paint at this point.

3 When the children are comfortable with using the brushes, start the final painting with black on another sheet of paper. Place the paper either vertically or horizontally. The monkeys may dance and move across the paper.

4 After the black paint is dry, use red paint to add the mouth, eyes, nose and other details.

Impasto painting

Age range: 7–11 years

Investigate texture in a painting by creating a still life using the medium of impasto.

Vocabulary

impasto   medium

still life   texture

Materials

- tempera paint (various colours)
- paste or dry soap flakes (grate a bar of soap)
- fruit or flowers
- cups
- spoon
- brushes (one for each colour)
- 23 x 30.5 cm cardboard
- pencil

Project notes

- Show prints of Vincent Van Gogh's work. Discuss how he used colour and texture to create these rich works of art.

- Explain that in the impasto technique, a paste-like substance is added to the paint to extend it while not changing the intensity of the colour. This is cost effective, as paints are expensive. Also, the thickness of the impasto adds texture to the painting and gives it more of a 3-D effect.

- Vincent Van Gogh's *Sunflowers* is an example of this type of painting.

Let's talk about it

- What is a still life?
- How is impasto different from watercolour?
- How does the thickness of the medium add to the feeling of the finished project?
- Does the subject seem more real or solid than it would if painted with watercolours? Why?
- Does the texture created from the impasto make the subject more interesting? How?

National Curriculum: Art & design
KS1: 1a, 1b, 2a, 2b, 2c, 4a, 4b, 4c, 5b, 5c
KS2: 1a, 1b, 2a, 2b, 2c, 4a, 4b, 4c, 5b, 5c
QCA Schemes of Work: Art & design
Unit 1B – Investigating materials
Unit 5A – Objects and meanings
Scottish 5–14 Guidelines: Art & design
Using materials, techniques, skills and media:
Investigating visually and recording; Using media;
Using visual elements
Expressing feelings, ideas, thoughts and solutions:
Creating and designing; Communicating

Step 1

Step 2

Step 3

Steps to follow

1 After discussing the impasto technique, set up a display of fruit or flowers for children to sketch on a piece of cardboard. Keep it simple.

2 Ask the children to paint the drawn picture with the impasto. Encourage them to leave the lumps as they paint. They should continue to paint until every part of the painting has been completed.

3 After the paint has dried, ask the children to outline the different parts of the painting with black tempera paint for more definition. The goal in this project is to gain experience in a very old medium and see how texture can add depth to a painting.

To mix impasto

Mix the impasto paint before starting. Let the children be involved in the process. Give small groups of children paints to share.

Mix tempera and paste or soap flakes in this ratio: half a cup (120 ml) tempera to third of a cup (80 g) paste or soap flakes. Leave the lumps to add texture to the painting. Make several cups of each colour.

Abstract watercolour

Age range: 7–11 years

Create an abstract painting by experimenting with several watercolour techniques.

Vocabulary

abstract

design

primary colours

secondary colours

technique

Materials

- scrap paper for practice
- 23 x 30.5 cm watercolour paper
- watercolour set with brush
- sponge
- straw
- cup for water
- tissue and paper towel
- cling film
- wax candle
- salt

Project notes

- Let children work at their own pace. Let them 'play' with all the techniques before they make their final picture. Encourage them to title their work. Children who feel unsure about creating art are often freed by abstract painting.

Let's talk about it

- How are abstract paintings different from realistic paintings?
- Abstract paintings may be a painting of an emotion or a sound. What emotion does your painting reflect?
- How are watercolour techniques used to create impressions of objects such as stars or feathers?

National Curriculum: Art & design
KS1: 1a, 2a, 2b, 2c, 4a, 4b, 5b, 5c
KS2: 1a, 2a, 2b, 2c, 4a, 4b, 5b, 5c
QCA Schemes of Work: Art & design
Unit 1B – Investigating materials
Unit 4A – Viewpoints
Scottish 5–14 Guidelines: Art & design
Using materials, techniques, skills and media:
Investigating visually and recording; Using
media; Using visual elements
Expressing feelings, ideas, thoughts
and solutions: Creating and designing.
Communicating

wet on wet   wet on dry

salt   blowing

cling film

sponge

gradated wash

Steps to follow

1 Model these watercolour techniques for the children:

• Sprinkle salt on wet paint. This will give a starry effect when dry.

• Cover wet paint with cling film and let it dry, then remove plastic to get a watery look.

• Dip a sponge in pigment and print on paper to create a lacy effect.

• Draw with a wax candle, then brush paint over the top for a 'resist' or masking technique.

• Blow across wet paint with a straw to get a spidery look.

• Wet the paper with clear water and then drop pigment into the pools for a feathery look called 'blooms'.

2 Ask the children to prime their paint sets by putting a drop of water on each colour to soften the pigment.

3 Allow the children enough time to try various techniques until they become relaxed and comfortable with them.

4 Ask the children to create an abstract painting using one or more of the techniques they have learned.

The colour wheel

Photocopy the colour wheel on page 23 for children. Ask them to colour in the wheel as you explain the meanings of the terms below.

Primary colours

Red, yellow and blue are called **PRIMARY** colours. Primary colours cannot be made by mixing colours together. You can use the primary colours to make other colours.

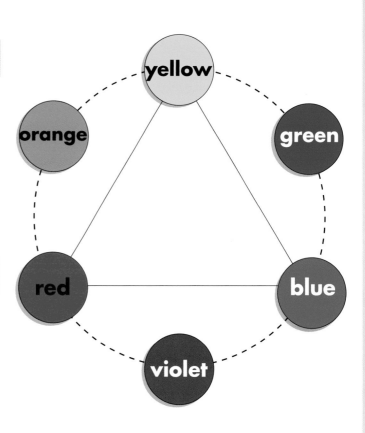

Secondary colours

Green, violet and orange are called **SECONDARY** colours. You can create the secondary colours by mixing two adjacent primary colours such as:

yellow + blue = green

blue + red = violet

red + yellow = orange

Complementary colours

Colours that are opposite one another on the colour wheel are called **COMPLEMENTARY** colours. These colour combinations are especially powerful when used together.

red – green

yellow – violet

blue – orange

Intermediate colours

INTERMEDIATE colours are yellow green, blue green, blue violet, red violet, red orange, and yellow orange. These colours are created by mixing each colour together such as:

yellow + green = yellow green

red + orange = red orange

blue + violet = blue violet

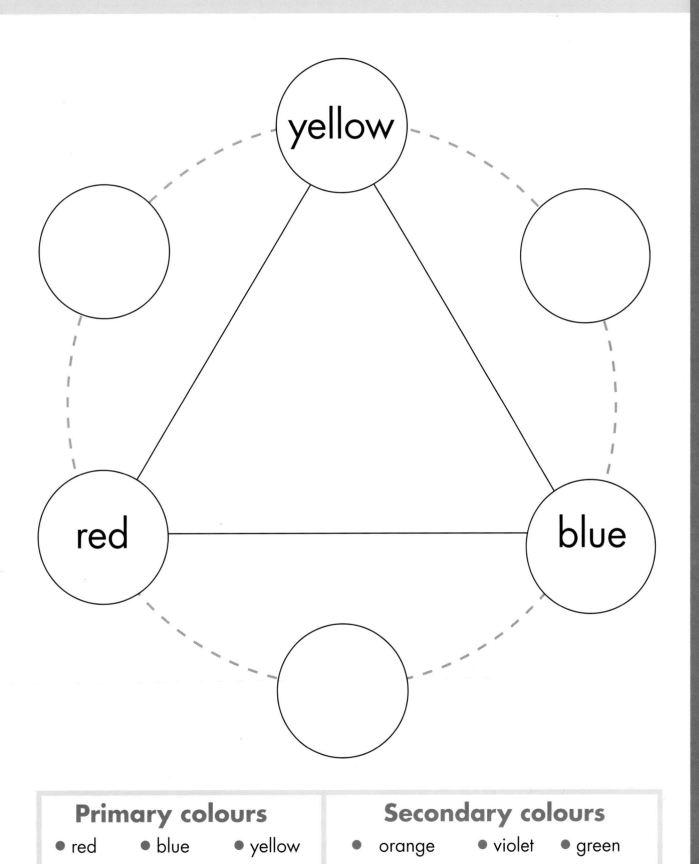

Primary colours			**Secondary colours**		
● red	● blue	● yellow	● orange	● violet	● green

Weaving

Weaving is an old craft used through the centuries by many different cultures to make textiles or objects. Using a variety of materials, a weaver can make textiles or objects in different patterns, textures, shapes and colours. Weaving textiles mainly uses the technique of weaving the weft material under and over the warp material. This is usually done on a frame such as a loom. Other weaving crafts use a form of braiding.

This chapter begins with a diagram and explanation of a basic loom and the use of the weft and warp. This gives children an initial understanding of the process and the basic techniques of weaving. The projects that follow concentrate on showing how different materials can be used in weaving. These include paper, woven strips, tissue paper, wool and raffia. Children can also develop skills in weaving three-dimensional objects such as a broom.

Weaving is a tactile and rewarding experience. As the children develop weaving skills, they can experiment with their own ideas and designs and build up a portfolio of work.

Contents

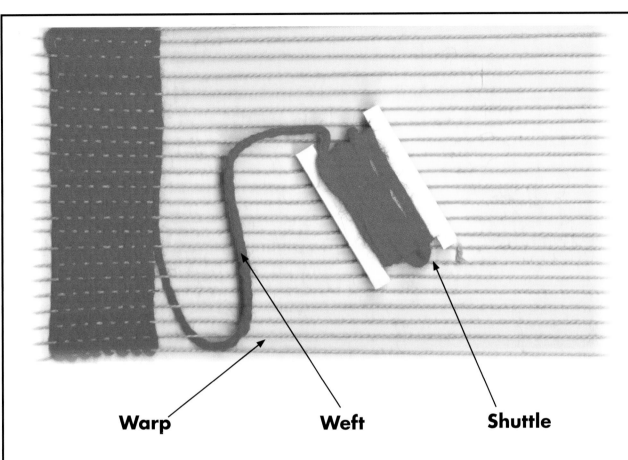

Warp　　　　　**Weft**　　　　**Shuttle**

Warp lines are threaded onto a loom.

Weft threads are wound onto a shuttle.

The **shuttle** passes over and under between the warp lines, creating the woven surface.

How to braid

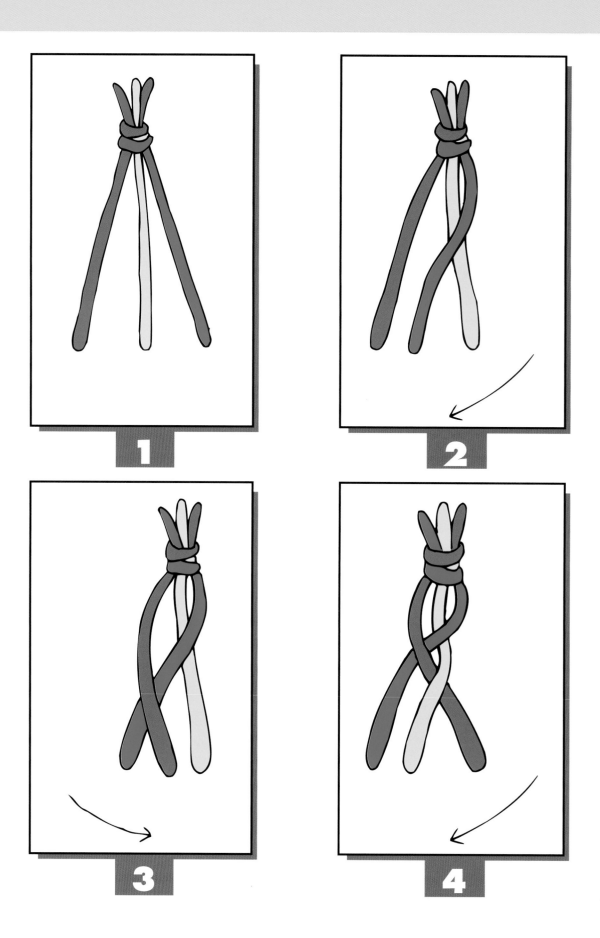

1

2

3

4

Creative Activities • Art and Design Projects • **www.scholastic.co.uk**

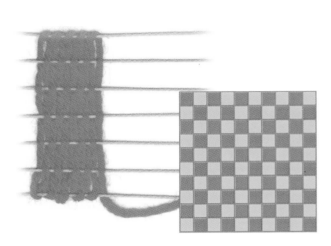

Regular weave

An even pattern is created in a woven piece by passing the weft **over** one warp and **under** the next.

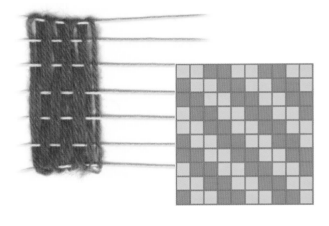

Twill weave

A diagonal pattern is created in a woven piece by passing the weft thread over one and under two or more warp threads.

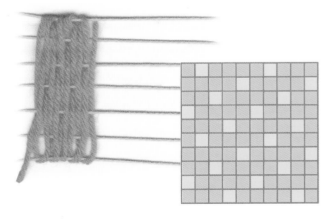

Satin weave

A smooth surface is created in the woven piece by passing the weft thread over several warp lines at a time.

Paper mats

Age range: 5–11 years

This basic project shows children how to weave a paper mat using complementary colours.

Vocabulary

complementary colours

weaving

warp

weft

Materials

- 23 x 30.5 cm card in red, green, yellow, purple, blue and orange – one sheet per child
- 2.5 x 23 cm strips of card – 11 per child (in a complementary colour to the main sheet)
- scissors
- glue or paste
- ruler
- pencil

Project notes

- Use these mats to decorate the room or as place mats for a class party.
- Explain a loom to the children. A loom is a device on which cloth is produced by interweaving thread or wool at right angles. The threads on the loom go in two different directions: vertically and horizontally. The vertical threads are called warp threads. The horizontal threads are called weft.

Let's talk about it

- How is weaving different from painting?
- What does weaving have in common with sculpture?
- What materials other than paper could you use to weave this project? (Explain how Native Americans, for example, used grasses to weave mats.)
- How did the use of complementary colours help in doing this project?

National Curriculum: Art & design
KS1: 2a, 2b, 4a, 4b, 5b, 5c
KS2: 2a, 2b, 4a, 4b, 5b, 5c
QCA Schemes of Work: Art & design
Unit 1B – Investigating materials
Unit 3B – Investigating pattern
Scottish 5–14 Guidelines: Art & design
Using materials, techniques, skills and media:
Using media; Using visual elements
Expressing feelings, ideas, thoughts
and solutions: Creating and designing;
Communicating

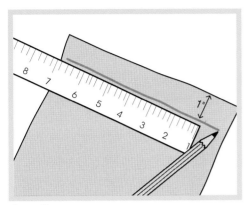

Step 2

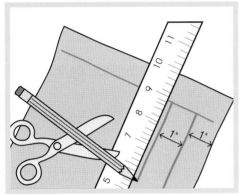

Step 3

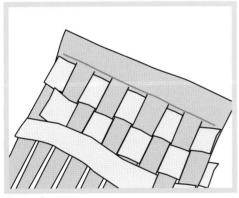

Step 4

Steps to follow

1 After discussing complementary colours (see below), let each child choose a sheet of card in one colour and 11 strips of paper in its complementary colour.

2 Lay the sheet of paper vertically on the table. Use a ruler to measure 2.5 cm from the top and mark with a pencil line. This will be where the cut lines will stop.

3 Measure across the width of the paper. Draw vertical lines every 2.5 cm. Cut on these lines. These cut lines will form the warp lines for this weaving.

4 Place the cut sheet of paper on the table and begin weaving with the pre-cut paper strips. Slide each woven strip up next to the previous one.

5 Carefully glue or paste the last strip to the warp ends to keep everything in place.

Complementary colours

Introduce the colour wheel (see page 23). Help the children to locate the complementary colours. Complementary colours are opposite each other

red – green

yellow – violet

blue – orange

Woven landscape

Irregular woven strips suggest landscape features. Children create an outdoor scene in the centre.

Vocabulary

landscape

warp

weaving

weft

Materials

- 23 x 30.5 cm sheets of card
- 13 x 2.5 cm card strips in two contrasting colours
- scissors
- crayons
- glue or paste
- ruler

Project notes

- Young children may need help measuring and making the initial cuts in the background paper.
- Offer a variety of coloured papers and let the children choose one sheet of paper for a background colour and contrasting strips of two other colours.

Let's talk about it

- What types of materials can be used in weaving?
- How can a weaving tell a story?
- How do the wavy cut lines add movement to the weaving?

National Curriculum: Art & design
KS1: 2a, 2b, 4a, 4b, 5b, 5c
KS2: 2a, 2b, 4a, 4b, 5b, 5c

QCA Schemes of Work: Art & design
Unit 1B – Investigating materials
Unit 3B – Investigating pattern
Unit 6C – A sense of place

Scottish 5–14 Guidelines: Art & design
Using materials, techniques, skills and media:
Investigating visually and recording; Using media; Using visual elements
Expressing feelings, ideas, thoughts and solutions: Creating and designing; Communicating

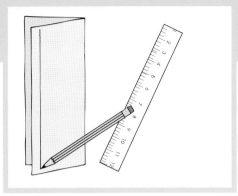

Step 1

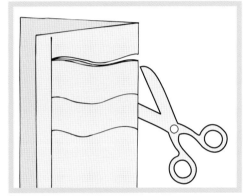

Step 2

Step 4

Steps 5 and 6

Steps to follow

1 Fold the sheet of card in half. Make a pencil line 2.5 cm from the open edge.

2 Starting at the fold, cut across the paper with curved lines. Stop at the pencil line each time. Cut approximately four lines in the top third and four lines in the bottom third of the paper. Do not make cuts in the centre.

3 Open the paper and lay it flat on the table. Smooth out the crease made when folding.

4 Draw and colour in a simple outdoor scene with crayon in the centre area of the paper – perhaps a tree and a house, or a sailboat with clouds and birds.

5 Begin weaving strips of paper through the slits. Use one colour of strips for the top and the other colour for the bottom. Do not cover the drawing.

6 Secure the paper strips with a drop of glue on each end when finished.

Tissue weaving

Age range: 5–11 years

Create a stained-glass window effect using transparent tissue paper and basic weaving skills.

Vocabulary

primary colours	transparent
secondary colours	warp
shuttle	weft

Materials

- 23 x 30.5 cm card for frames
- 23 x 30.5 cm white paper
- scissors
- ruler
- 5 x 30.5 cm tissue paper strips – one blue, one red, one yellow
- 5 x 23 cm tissue paper strips – one blue, two red, two yellow
- glue or paste

Project notes

- Pre-cut the frames for younger children (see step 5).

Let's talk about it

- How are new colours created in this weaving technique?
- Can weaving coloured wools side by side appear to be an illusion of different colours? (The eye seems able to mix colour all on its own. Red wool woven next to a yellow wool can create orange when viewed from a distance.)

National Curriculum: Art & design
KS1: 2a, 2b, 4a, 4b, 5b, 5c
KS2: 2a, 2b, 4a, 4b, 5b, 5c
QCA Schemes of Work: Art & design
Unit 1B – Investigating materials
Unit 3B – Investigating pattern
Scottish 5–14 Guidelines: Art & design
Using materials, techniques, skills and media:
Using media; Using visual elements
Expressing feelings, ideas, thoughts
and solutions: Creating and designing.
Communicating

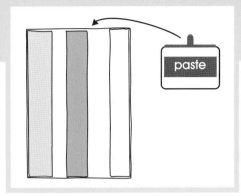

Step 2

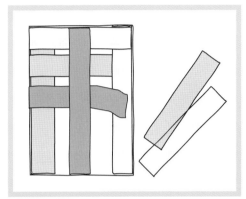

Step 3

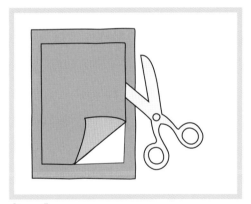

Step 5

Steps to follow

1 Start by placing the white paper vertically on the table.

2 Glue one red, one blue and one yellow 30.5 cm strip side by side, starting at the top of the paper, to create the warp. Glue down only the tops.

3 Start weaving the shorter coloured strips through the warp, starting with yellow and continuing with red, then blue, red again, and finishing with yellow. These are the weft. Glue the ends of each strip to the white paper to keep them in place.

4 When all strips are woven and glued in place, glue the bottom of the warp pieces to the bottom of the paper.

5 Mark a 2.5 cm border around the outside edge of the coloured card. Cut on this line to create a frame for the picture.

6 Place the frame piece over the woven paper and glue in place.

7 Hold the finished project up to the light to see how mixing two primary colours will result in a secondary colour wherever the two cross one another. Red and yellow woven together will produce orange. Yellow and blue will produce green. Blue and red will produce purple.

Step 6

Art folders

Make an art portfolio from woven corrugated paper.

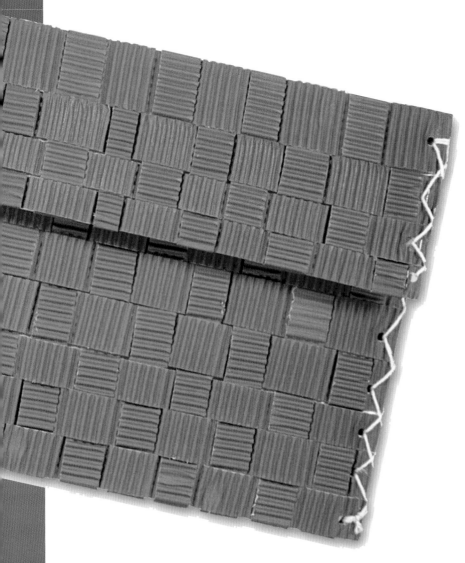

Vocabulary

texture

warp

weft

Materials

- corrugated display board cut into 5 x 56 cm and 5 x 71 cm strips
- 56 x 71 cm card – one per child
- stapler
- glue gun with glue (optional)
- hole punch
- thick wool

Project notes

- A lot of space is needed to work on this project, so try sitting on the floor to work.

Let's talk about it

- What types of materials can be used to weave?
- What is the loom in this project?
- How does the texture help in creating a pattern on the portfolio?
- How is sewing like weaving?

National Curriculum: Art & design
KS1: 2a, 2b, 4a, 4b, 5b, 5c
KS2: 2a, 2b, 4a, 4b, 5b, 5c
QCA Schemes of Work: Art & design
Unit 1B – Investigating materials
Unit 3B – Investigating pattern
Scottish 5–14 Guidelines: Art & design
Using materials, techniques, skills and media:
Using media; Using visual elements
Expressing feelings, ideas, thoughts
and solutions: Creating and designing.
Communicating

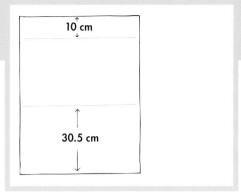

Step 1

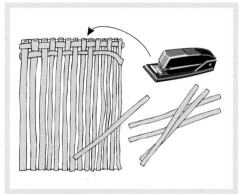

Steps 2 and 3

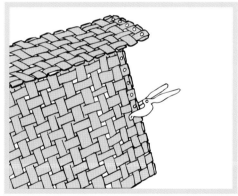

Steps 5 and 6

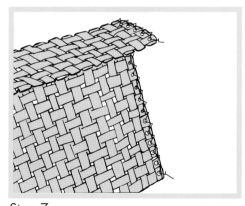

Step 7

Steps to follow

1 Place the card vertically on a flat surface. Measure 10 cm down from the top and draw a line. This will be the flap. Then draw a line 30.5 cm up from the bottom. This will be the fold to create the pocket of the portfolio. Flip the card over, keeping it vertical.

2 Staple the long strips of paper, corrugated side up, side by side to the top and bottom of the card. Let any extra paper hang over the top edge.

3 Begin weaving the shorter weft strips, smooth side up, back and forth through the warp strips. Staple each strip in place after it is pushed close together. A checkerboard pattern of textures should be visible.

4 After the weaving is complete, flip it over and turn down any pieces hanging over the top of the folder. Glue or staple these pieces in place.

5 Fold the folder on the line drawn 30.5 cm from the bottom, leaving the flap up.

6 While holding the sides together, punch holes through both layers along both sides. An adult will need to punch the holes for younger children, as it takes some strength to go through both layers of woven paper.

7 Tie a strip of heavy wool to one side and sew the sides together. Complete both sides. Fold the flap portion down to close the folder.

Woven bookmarks

Age range: 7–11 years

Make a wool bookmark using basic weaving skills.

Vocabulary

loom	warp
patterning	weft
shuttle	

Materials

- cardboard loom (see below)
- wool cut in 2.25 m lengths, two different colours per child
- plastic forks, one per child
- scissors
- metrestick

Project notes

- If possible, show weavings from different cultures. You may wish to use this project as part of a lesson on different cultures.

- Show photographs or pictures of different types of weaving from other cultures. Use the local library and the internet as sources of information.

Making cardboard looms:

- Cut cardboard into 13 x 20 cm looms. Use a pair of scissors to cut at least six 0.5 cm notches in each end.

Let's talk about it

- How is this cardboard loom different from a loom used for making a rug?
- How do the colour and texture of the materials make a weaving different from a painting?
- What are the similarities between painting and weaving?

National Curriculum: Art & design
KS1: 2a, 2b, 4a, 4b, 4c, 5b, 5c
KS2: 2a, 2b, 4a, 4b, 4c, 5b, 5c
QCA Schemes of Work: Art & design
Unit 1B – Investigating materials
Unit 3B – Investigating pattern
Scottish 5–14 Guidelines: Art & design
Using materials, techniques, skills and media:
Using media; Using visual elements
Expressing feelings, ideas, thoughts
and solutions: Creating and designing.
Communicating

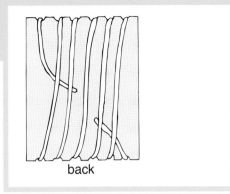

back

Step 2

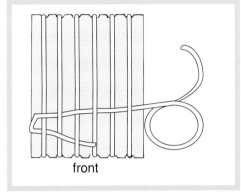

front

Step 3

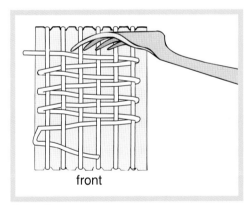

front

Step 5

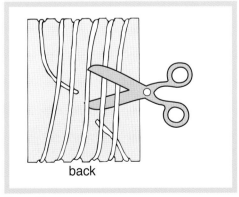

back

Step 7

Steps to follow

1 Tape the metrestick on the table next to the wool. Let the children choose the colours they wish to use. They should measure the wool along the measuring stick and cut the pieces into 2.25 m lengths. Use one colour wool for the warp and another colour for the weft.

2 Attach the wool to the loom by holding the end with one finger about halfway and wrapping from top to bottom, making sure to slide wool into each notch. Make the tension firm but not rigid. (When the weaving is finished, you may cut this warp string, leaving a few centimetres so it will not unravel.)

3 Begin the weaving process by attaching the weft wool. Start in the middle of the warp and weave the wool in and out of the warp strings using your finger as the shuttle to carry the wool.

4 Proceed to weave. Work the wool back and forth through the warp, alternating rows over and under on each new pass.

5 After each pass, pack down the wool gently with the fork.

6 When the weaving is complete, weave the last bit of wool back through the warp, ending in the centre. This keeps the wool from unravelling without spoiling the weaving with a knot.

7 To remove the weaving from the loom, turn the loom over and cut the warp strings in the centre. Use a bit of extra wool to tie the strings together with a knot on each end.

Paper baskets

Age range: 5–11 years

Weave a basket using a monochromatic colour scheme.

Vocabulary

monochromatic

warp

weaving

weft

Materials

- 22.5 x 22.5 cm card
- 2.5 x 33 cm card strips
- glue or paste
- ruler
- pencil
- scissors
- stapler

Project notes

- These baskets are small enough to be useful and don't take up too much space. Use the baskets in the classroom for small items such as crayons or chalk.

Let's talk about it

- How is weaving a basket different from weaving a blanket?
- How are they the same?
- How are variations created even in a monochromatic colour scheme?

National Curriculum: Art & design
KS1: 2a, 2b, 4a, 4b, 5b, 5c
KS2: 2a, 2b, 4a, 4b, 5b, 5c
QCA Schemes of Work: Art & design
Unit 1B – Investigating materials
Unit 3B – Investigating pattern
Unit 5B – Containers
Scottish 5–14 Guidelines: Art & design
Using materials, techniques, skills and media:
Using media; Using visual elements
Expressing feelings, ideas, thoughts
and solutions: Creating and designing;
Communicating

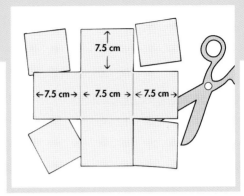

Step 1

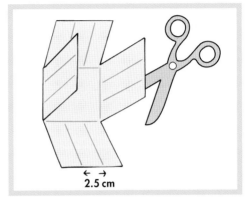

Step 2

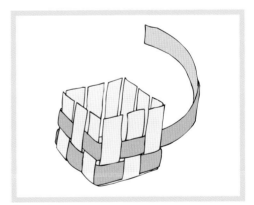

Step 4

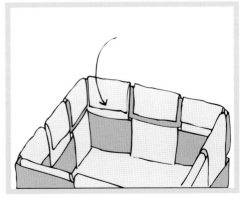

Step 5

Steps to follow

1 Lay the sheet of paper flat on the table. Use a ruler to measure 7.5 cm from each edge of the paper. Draw a line at each of these points. Cut out the corner boxes.

2 The four pieces of paper sticking out will create the sides of the basket. Measure each section into 2.5 cm strips and cut from the outer edge to the centre line. There will be three 2.5 cm strips on each side attached to the centre square.

3 Fold these strips up to form the sides of the basket. This is the warp.

4 The 2.5 x 33 cm strips will be the weft. Start at a bottom corner and weave in and out between the warp strips. Glue the ends together after each row to keep them in place. Continue weaving until you reach the top of the basket.

5 You may fold the top edges of the warp over to the inside and glue them down. To make a more finished edge, glue an extra strip inside the top edge.

6 If desired, staple on a paper handle.

What is a monochromatic colour scheme?

Monochromatic refers to the use of a single colour in an art project. That colour, however, may be of several different intensities. Children may choose to use light and dark green or two shades of blue. It is important to realise that even a monochromatic colour scheme can be interesting and varied.

Broom art

Age range: 7–11 years

Learn three-dimensional weaving techniques by making a broom.

Vocabulary

shuttle

reef knot

warp

weft

Materials

- broom straw cut in varying lengths from 30 cm to 40 cm

- strong garden shears or scissors

- twine, wool or sisal cut in 76 cm and 61 cm lengths

Project notes

- Brooms may be made from straw, cornhusks, wheat straw, or any type of tall grass.

- Secure the straw clusters with rubber bands or clothes pins while weaving. Remove them when the weaving is finished.

Let's talk about it

- Making brooms is an old art form that has almost been forgotten. Many years ago, broom makers developed techniques to create brooms for every different household task.

- What other materials might they have used in making brooms?

- What acted as a loom in this project?

- What was the weft, warp, and shuttle?

National Curriculum: Art & design
KS1: 2a, 2b, 4a, 4b, 4c, 5b, 5c
KS2: 2a, 2b, 4a, 4b, 4c, 5b, 5c
QCA Schemes of Work: Art & design
Unit 1B – Investigating materials
Scottish 5–14 Guidelines: Art & design
Using materials, techniques, skills and media:
Using media; Using visual elements
Expressing feelings, ideas, thoughts
and solutions: Creating and designing;
Communicating

Steps 1 & 2

Step 3

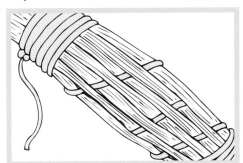

Step 4

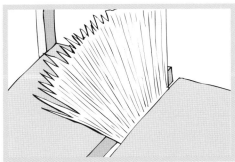

Step 5

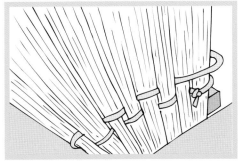

Step 6

Steps to follow

1 Gather a bundle of broom straw. Tap the straw on the table to get one end of the bundle flat and even. Use the 76 cm piece of twine and tie it 13 cm from the flat end. Tie the straw together with a reef knot (see page 42).

2 Now wrap the twine four times around the bundle of straw. As you wrap, move back toward the flat end. This is the beginning of the broom handle.

3 Separate the handle into seven clusters and begin the weaving. Wrap the twine over and under the clusters of straw. Work back toward the end of the handle.

4 Approximately 5 cm from the end, wrap the twine around the handle four times and make a knot. Leave enough twine for a loop to hang the broom.

5 Flatten the broom end between two chairs. Use fingers to separate the broom into five sections.

6 Weave the 61 cm piece of twine in and out between the sections. Weave the twine several times across the broom. Tie a knot to hold the twine in place. Children may add a second row of weaving to add extra strength to the broom.

7 Trim the broom end with garden shears or scissors.

How to tie a reef knot

▶ SCHOLASTIC

PHOTOCOPIABLE

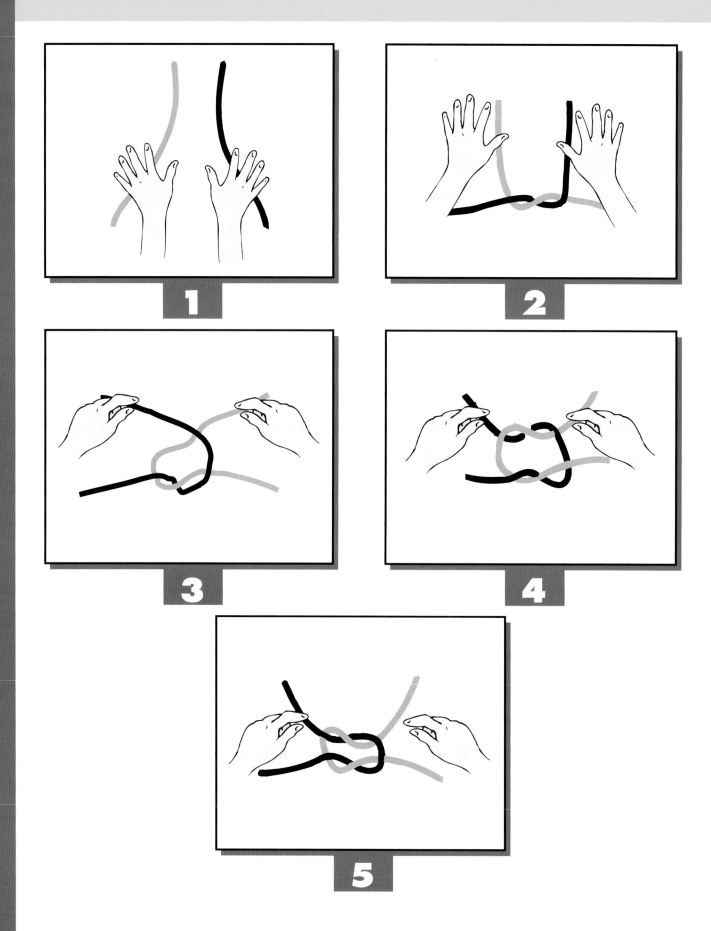

Printing

Printing is an art form where an image is transferred by means of ink or paint to another surface. The printing tool itself creates the image. All sorts of objects can be used as printing tools, for example the cross sections of a green pepper or a simple piece of string. Designs can also be carved onto objects like blocks of wood of potatoes. The nice thing about printing tools is that they can be used again and again.

A wide range of printing tools is used in this chapter including bubbles, feathers, fish, stencils, string and rubbers. Each printing project looks at ways of producing an effective print by different media. These include the use of monoprints, mixed media, and the use of different colour combinations and patterns.

Printing is valuable in teaching the basic principles of design. Children learn to repeat shapes and colours to build interesting patterns. Whatever the type of printing, allow the children plenty of time to explore different design possibilities when creating a printed picture. Printing is a particularly satisfying medium for children in both key stages because they can produce immediate images with a sense of achievement.

Contents

Monoprints

Age range: 5–11 years

A monoprint is made by pressing a sheet of paper onto a surface where paint or ink is smeared.

Vocabulary

monoprint

printing

Materials

- 30.5 x 46 cm plain white paper
- tempera paint (various colours)
- paintbrush for each colour
- masking tape
- paper towels for clean-up
- smooth, sealed-surface table or counter top

Project notes

- Be sure the printing area is clean and clear of obstruction. Provide as many work areas as space permits. Adult supervision is advisable during printing.
- Children may need smocks.
- Children should work in pairs to manipulate the paper as they print. Both children should sign the print.
- The paper should not be moved once it is placed on the painted area.

Let's talk about it

- What is the proper way to handle materials and to cooperate while doing a monoprint with a partner?
- What are the differences between printing and painting?

National Curriculum: Art & design
KS1: 2a, 2b, 4a, 4b, 5b, 5c
KS2: 2a, 2b, 2c, 4a, 4b, 5b, 5c
QCA Schemes of Work: Art & design
Unit 1B – Investigating materials
Unit 3B – Investigating pattern
Unit 4A – Viewpoints
Scottish 5–14 Guidelines: Art & design
Using materials, techniques, skills and media:
Using media; Using visual elements
Expressing feelings, ideas, thoughts
and solutions: Creating and designing;
Communicating

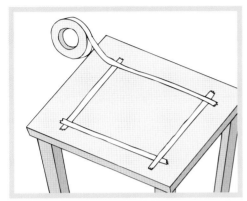

Step 1

Step 2

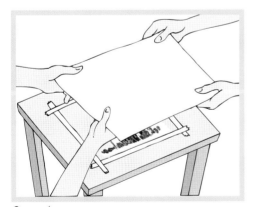

Step 4

Steps to follow

1 Mask off a 30.5 x 46 cm area on a smooth table surface.

2 Using tempera paint and brushes, paint a picture in this area.

3 Ask each child to choose a partner to help make a print of this tabletop painting.

4 The partners should lift opposite sides of the paper and gently lay it over the top of the painting on the table. They should then gently press down over the entire paper without rubbing.

5 Lift the paper to see that the paint has transferred to the underside of the paper. Set the print aside to dry.

6 Clean off the table and prepare for the next pair of children.

Bubble prints

Age range: 5–11 years

Create a print using, of all things, soap bubbles!

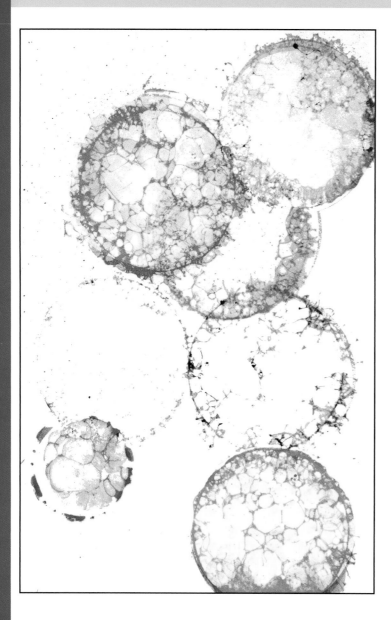

Vocabulary

primary colours

printing

secondary colours

Materials

- 23 x 30.5 cm white paper
- water
- liquid dishwashing detergent
- tempera paint
- plastic straws
- plastic cups or bowls
- paper towels
- measuring cup

Project notes

- Set up a workstation for small groups of children.
- Plan ahead for a place to put wet projects to dry.
- Ask an older child or an adult to blow the bubbles for younger children. For safety, use non-toxic paints and detergent.

Let's talk about it

- What are primary and secondary colours?
- Why is a white paper background preferable for this type of project?

National Curriculum: Art & design
KS1: 2a, 2b, 4a, 4b, 5b, 5c
KS2: 2a, 2b, 2c, 4a, 4b, 5b, 5c
QCA Schemes of Work: Art & design
Unit 1B – Investigating materials
Unit 3B – Investigating pattern
Unit 4A – Viewpoints
Scottish 5-14 Guidelines: Art & design
Using materials, techniques, skills and media:
Using media; Using visual elements
Expressing feelings, ideas, thoughts
and solutions: Creating and designing;
Communicating

Steps to follow

1 Children may need to experiment with this technique on a piece of scrap paper before they begin their final project. They also need to see which of the colours of paint they prefer to use in their print.

2 Place the straw in the bubble mixture and blow. Blow until bubbles extend up past the lip of the cup or bowl. Remove the straw.

3 Place a sheet of paper gently over the bubbles. Wait for the bubbles to pop.

4 Lift the paper and marvel at the result. Set the paper aside and let it dry.

5 Children may add more prints to the page and experiment with designs and colour combinations. Let the prints dry in between colour changes.

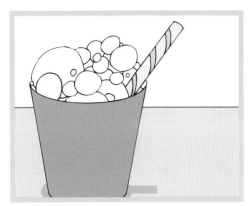

Step 2

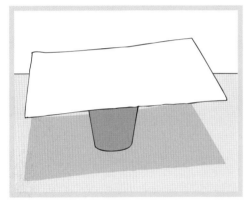

Step 3

How to make the bubble mixture

Mix water, paint and detergent in equal parts in cups or bowls.

Troubleshooting hints:

- If the mixture bubbles but does not go past the rim of the cup, add water.
- If the mixture does not bubble at all, add detergent.
- If the bubbles are too faint, add paint.

Soft rubbings

Age range: 7–11 years

Create a print using pastel chalk and a stencil then add details of buildings, fish, plants or animals.

Vocabulary

colour scheme   pastels

cool colours   stencil

fixative   warm colours

Materials

- 23 x 30.5 cm white paper
- newspaper
- pastel chalks
- 5 x 30.5 cm cardboard strips
- cotton wool balls (two or three per child)
- scissors
- black fine-tip marker (one per child)
- black ink pad
- spray fixative

Project notes

- Pre-cut the stencils for younger children.
- Children can find inspiration in the shapes around them: the rectangular shapes of buildings or the curving shapes of mountain ranges and rippling water. Stencil cuts should be kept simple.
- Offer clean cotton wool balls after each colour change so colours don't get mixed and muddied.
- Spray fixatives should be used in a well-ventilated area and by adults only.

Let's talk about it

- Why is the choice of colour scheme important?
- Why are some colours referred to as cool and others as warm?
- Why is the use of a fixative necessary with this medium?

National Curriculum: Art & design
KS1: 2a, 2b, 4a, 4b, 5b, 5c
KS2: 2a, 2b, 2c, 4a, 4b, 5b, 5c

QCA Schemes of Work: Art & design
Unit 1B – Investigating materials
Unit 3B – Investigating pattern
Unit 4A – Viewpoints

Scottish 5–14 Guidelines: Art & design
Using materials, techniques, skills and media:
Using media; Using visual elements
Expressing feelings, ideas, thoughts
and solutions: Creating and designing;
Communicating

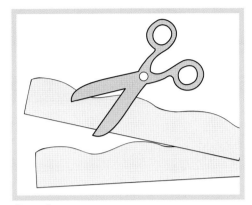

Step 1

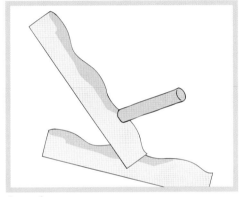

Step 2

Step 3

Steps to follow

1 Cut varying shapes along one long edge of each cardboard strip.

2 Lay the first stencil piece on newspaper and cover the cut edge with a layer of chalk.

3 Place that stencil in the desired spot on the white paper and hold firmly. Using a cotton wool ball, brush the chalk onto the paper. Lift the stencil carefully to see the design.

4 Continue this process with the other stencil strips until the entire paper is covered. Use a new strip for each colour of chalk.

5 Use the ink pad and black marker to add details such as animals, trees, buildings and people. Press a fingertip on the ink pad and then press the finger onto the paper. Outline and add detail to each resulting figure with the marker.

6 Spray the final project with fixative to prevent smudges.

Let's talk about colour schemes

• Cool colours such as blues, purples and greens can suggest oceans or mountains.

• Warm colours such as oranges, yellows and reds can suggest desert landscapes or sunsets.

Fantasy fowl

Age range: 5–11 years

Use materials found in nature and the classroom to make birds with colourful plumage.

Vocabulary

fantasy

printing

realistic

Materials

- various colours of tempera paint in cups
- tempera paint on paper plates
- paintbrush for each colour
- paper towels
- cotton bud (one per child)
- 30.5 x 46 cm card
- feathers (several per child)
- broad-tip marker

Project notes

- Set up materials so that the children can work in small groups. Ask the children to wear smocks or old shirts.

- After applying paint to feathers, separate the feather parts to help keep the feather look. Never saturate the feather with paint or the texture will be lost. Replace soggy feathers with fresh ones.

- Show paintings and photographs of realistic birds. Observe the many colours and shapes of feathers. Discuss how realistic bird paintings differ from your fantasy print.

National Curriculum: Art & design
KS1: 2a, 2b, 4a, 4b, 5b, 5c
KS2: 2a, 2b, 2c, 4a, 4b, 5b, 5c
QCA Schemes of Work: Art & design
Unit 1B – Investigating materials
Unit 2B – Mother Nature, designer
Unit 4A – Viewpoints
Scottish 5–14 Guidelines: Art & design
Using materials, techniques, skills and media:
Investigating visually and recording; Using media;
Using visual elements
Expressing feelings, ideas, thoughts and solutions:
Creating and designing; Communicating

Let's talk about it

- What other types of nature objects can be used to make prints?
- How do designs change from an original idea to the finished product?
- Would it be easier to paint a picture of a bird or to print one using this method?

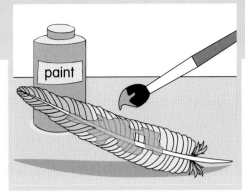

Step 2

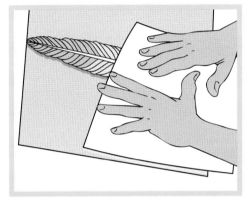

Step 3

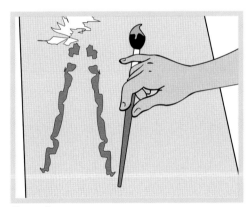

Step 5

Steps 6 and 7

Steps to follow

1 Think about what this fantasy fowl will look like, then decide whether the paper will be used horizontally or vertically. Children may want to lightly pencil in a simple drawing of a bird as a guideline.

2 Paint one side of a feather and place it paint-side down on the paper. Encourage the children to work from the top to the bottom of the design to avoid smudging.

3 Place a paper towel on top of the feather and press gently. Remove the towel and gently lift the feather to see the print.

4 Continue printing with new feathers until the bird's body is complete. Set the paper aside to dry.

5 When prints are dry, lay a paintbrush handle down in one of the plates of tempera to coat one side. Use the brush handle to print legs on the bird.

6 While the legs are drying, dip a cotton bud in tempera and print the eyes.

7 After the paint is dry, use a broad-tip marker to make the feet and a beak.

Go fish

Age range: 5–11 years

Using mixed media, children create an underwater scene showing dimension and movement.

Vocabulary

background

foreground

mixed media

Materials

- 23 x 30.5 cm or 30.5 x 46 cm white drawing paper
- small fresh fish
- black tempera paint or printer's ink
- paint roller or brush
- newspaper
- cotton wool balls
- paper towels

Project notes

- This project can be done by children of all ages and is a good one to do in small groups.
- Select small fish that will fit on the paper without filling the page. Choose fish that are fresh and in good shape.
- Show how objects slightly to the right or left of centre make the object appear to be entering or leaving the scene.

Let's talk about it

- What is mixed media?
- Does the artwork show movement and depth?
- Locate foreground, middle ground and background objects.

National Curriculum: Art & design
KS1: 2a, 2b, 4a, 4b, 4c, 5b, 5c
KS2: 2a, 2b, 2c, 4a, 4b, 4c, 5b, 5c

QCA Schemes of Work: Art & design
Unit 1B – Investigating materials
Unit 3B – Investigating pattern
Unit 4A – Viewpoints

Scottish 5–14 Guidelines: Art & design
Using materials, techniques, skills and media:
Investigating visually and recording; Using media;
Using visual elements
Expressing feelings, ideas, thoughts and solutions:
Creating and designing; Communicating

Step 1

Step 2

Step 4

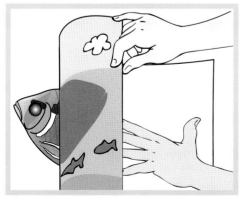

Steps 5 and 6

Steps to follow

1 Sketch an underwater scene on the paper. Colour the page completely with crayon. Encourage the children to fill the page with all the things one might find underwater.

2 Squeeze paint or ink onto a smooth surface. Spread it evenly with a paint roller until the roller is coated evenly with paint or ink. If a paint roller and ink are not available, a brush and tempera paint may be used.

3 Blot excess moisture from the fish with a paper towel. Stuff tiny bits of cotton wool or paper towel under the gill and lateral fin of the fish so they will print clearly. Place the fish on a sheet of newspaper.

4 Roll or brush ink or paint over the fish, starting with the head and working toward the tail. Try not to get too much ink or paint under the scales. Lift the fish gently and place it on a clean sheet of newspaper.

5 Check the coloured drawing and decide where the fish print will go. Place the drawing paper upside down on the inked fish. Starting at the centre of the fish, rub gently over the paper with the fingers, moving toward the edges of the fish.

6 Gently peel the paper from the fish and let it dry.

String prints

Age range: 5–11 years

Make a string print in 'relief' style. The theme could tie in with a subject being studied in class.

Vocabulary

relief print

texture

Materials

- string or wool
- white glue
- 13 x 20 cm thick cardboard
- paint roller
- tempera paint
- scrap paper
- 23 x 30.5 cm card
- pencil

Project notes

- Use a good-quality string that will hold up to the wet paint.
- Keep the design simple.
- Be sure the string is securely attached to the cardboard.
- Work with small groups and monitor the amount of paint being used. The paint should completely cover the roller in a thin, even coat.

Let's talk about it

- What is a relief print?
- How does the print differ from the original design on the cardboard?
- How does this string print give the impression of texture?

National Curriculum: Art & design
KS1: 2a, 2b, 4a, 4b, 5b, 5c
KS2: 2a, 2b, 2c, 4a, 4b, 5b, 5c

QCA Schemes of Work: Art & design
Unit 1B – Investigating materials
Unit 3B – Investigating pattern
Unit 4A – Viewpoints
Unit 6C – A sense of place

Scottish 5–14 Guidelines: Art & design
Using materials, techniques, skills and media:
Using media; Using visual elements
Expressing feelings, ideas, thoughts and solutions:
Creating and designing

Steps 1 and 2

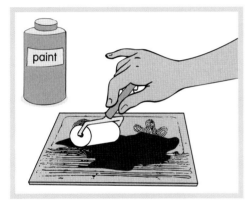

Step 5

Step 6

Steps to follow

1 Sketch a simple design on the cardboard.

2 Put a line of glue along the design outline. Lay string along the line of glue. Fill in the design with glue and lay in string until the design is completely filled in.

3 When the design has been filled in with string, let it dry completely.

4 Squirt tempera paint on a flat surface. Roll the paint roller in the tempera until it is completely coated.

5 Gently roll the coated paint roller over the string design, being careful not to dislodge the string. Do not saturate the string with paint. A little paint is sufficient.

6 Place the scrap paper over the design and rub gently. Peel off the paper to view the print.

7 When the children are satisfied with the print on the scrap paper, they may print the design on the card. Repaint the string as needed.

Name chop

Age range: 5–11 years

Introduce children to the name chop, a traditional way of signing a work of art in Asian countries.

Vocabulary

name chop

Materials

- foam trays cut into 5 x 8 cm rectangles
- pencils
- tempera paint (various colours)
- paintbrushes
- 5 x 8 cm scrap paper
- 23 x 30.5 cm card

Project notes

- Wash the foam trays with soap and water to help the paint stick better.
- Let the children use their name chops to sign their own stories, paintings and projects.
- This process may also be used to make prints of animals and plants.

Let's talk about it

- How is printing different in different cultures?
- Why was the printing process an important development in history?
- What everyday items are the product of a printing process?

National Curriculum: Art & design
KS1: 2a, 2b, 4a, 4b, 4c, 5b, 5c
KS2: 2a, 2b, 2c, 4a, 4b, 4c, 5b, 5c
QCA Schemes of Work: Art & design
Unit 1B – Investigating materials
Unit 3B – Investigating pattern
Unit 4A – Viewpoints
Unit 6C – A sense of place
Scottish 5–14 Guidelines: Art & design
Using materials, techniques, skills and media:
Using media; Using visual elements
Expressing feelings, ideas, thoughts
and solutions: Creating and designing;
Communicating

Step 1

Step 2

Step 3

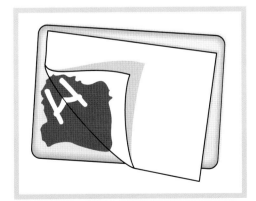

Step 4

Steps to follow

1 Give each child a piece of foam block, a small piece of scrap paper, and a pencil. Ask them to print their names clearly and firmly on the paper.

2 Place the scrap paper facedown on the block. If the name has been written firmly enough, it will be visible through the paper. Now trace over the letters to press them into the block. The letters are now written on the block backwards.

3 Lightly paint the surface of the block with tempera paint. Experiment to discover what level of paint coverage is the most effective.

4 Gently press the name chop onto a piece of scrap paper as a test. Lift the name chop to see the print. The name should be clearly shown.

5 Apply a new coat of paint. Print on the card a number of times to create a pattern. Wipe off the name chop between prints.

Rubber stamp

Age range: 7–11 years

Create a rubber stamp to use as a signature stamp or on cards, gift tags and bookmarks.

Vocabulary

medium

negative space

positive space

printing

Materials

- scrap paper
- pencil
- printing block (approximately 5 x 8 cm) or large rubber erasers
- broad-tipped watercolour markers
- carving tools
- stencils or small biscuit cutters
- card

Project notes

- When demonstrating with the carving tool, always point out safety rules:
  - Keep your free hand back from the cutter and close to your body.
  - Carve away from the body.
  - Carve away only small bits at a time.
- Use watercolour markers so colour may be removed easily with water. Clean off the printing medium with a damp towel before changing colour.
- Keep the design simple. Do not use letters.
- Work quickly when printing so the marker doesn't dry.

Let's talk about it

- What is the proper way to handle carving tools?
- Talk about positive and negative space.

National Curriculum: Art & design
KS1: 2a, 2b, 4a, 4b, 5b, 5c
KS2: 2a, 2b, 2c, 4a, 4b, 5b, 5c

QCA Schemes of Work: Art & design
Unit 1B – Investigating materials
Unit 3B – Investigating pattern
Unit 4A – Viewpoints

Scottish 5–14 Guidelines: Art & design
Using materials, techniques, skills and media:
Using media; Using visual elements
Expressing feelings, ideas, thoughts
and solutions: Creating and designing;
Communicating

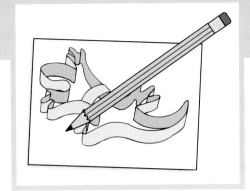

Step 1

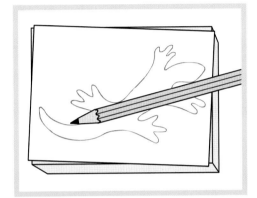

Step 2

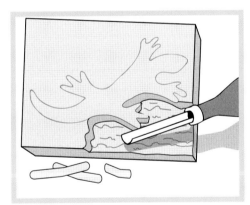

Step 3

Steps to follow

1 Make a design on scrap paper by tracing around the stencil or biscuit cutter. Retrace the image firmly so it can be seen through the back of the sheet of paper.

2 Turn the scrap paper over onto the print block material. Retrace the image to create an outline on the block. Determine which is the positive part of the design and which is the negative or surrounding space.

3 Use a carving tool to carve out the design. Decide whether to carve out the positive or the negative area of the design.

4 Spread watercolour marker on the printing surface of the block. Turn the block over quickly and print on the scrap paper.

5 When the children are comfortable with printing, they may print on the final paper. Let them experiment with various ways to fill a sheet of paper by using the same design over and over again. How can various colour combinations affect the final result?

Positive or negative?

The same design might be carved on both sides of the block.
One side will have the positive (the background) cut out and the other side will have the negative (the figure or design) cut out.
Line up the block with the edge of the paper and print one design beside the other by flipping the block over and lining it up.

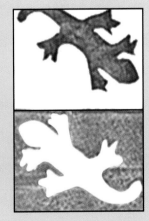

Clay

Clay has been used to make objects by many cultures throughout the ages. Clay is a very malleable material and can be moulded and shaped into everyday objects such as tiles, pots and cups or into art forms such as sculptures.

The projects in this chapter illustrate ways of making clay tiles, a range of pots and vases, beads and simple clay sculptures. The projects cover a range of techniques for working with clay. These include moulding, rolling, pinching and pulling, joining clay parts together and creating interesting textures on a clay surface.

Using clay in class allows children to experiment and develop skills in manipulating a soft material into many different shapes and objects, using techniques such as rolling, pinching, pulling, pressing and coiling. Children can use tools to create patterns and different textures onto the clay. They can also see at first hand how clay changes its appearance after it is fired or dried out.

Contents

Types of pottery

There are many types of pottery:

Pinch pots

Pinch pots seem to be the easiest for young children or those who have never crafted with clay before, since absolutely nothing can go wrong.

Coil pots

Coil pots are a favourite as they can be any shape you desire and most children love to make the long snake-like coils.

Slab pots

Slab pots are equally easy but look quite different from pinch or coil pottery.

Hand-thrown pots

Hand-thrown pots are shaped on a potter's wheel with the hands and water while the wheel is spinning. Many ceramic and pottery classes teach this technique.

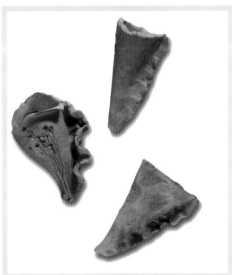

Faux fossils

Age range: 5–11 years

Create fossil look-alikes while learning the techniques of working with clay.

Vocabulary

fixative

kiln

Materials

- clay
- newspaper
- cardboard with clean paper cover
- rolling pin
- objects to make imprints such as shells, leaves, flowers and plastic fish
- magnets (optional)
- spray fixative (optional)
- access to a kiln

Project notes

- For easy clean-up, cover the work surface with newspaper. Always work the clay on a piece of cardboard with a clean paper cover.
- Don't be concerned about the shape of the fossils.
- Glue a magnet on the back to make a unique fridge magnet.

Let's talk about it

- How are real fossils created?
- How is this clay different from clays made of plastic?

National Curriculum: Art & design
KS1: 2a, 2b, 4a, 4b, 5b, 5c
KS2: 2a, 2b, 2c, 4a, 4b, 5b, 5c
QCA Schemes of Work: Art & design
Unit 1C – What is sculpture?
Scottish 5–14 Guidelines: Art & design
Using materials, techniques, skills and media:
Investigating visually and recording; Using
media; Using visual elements
Expressing feelings, ideas, thoughts
and solutions: Creating and designing.
Communicating

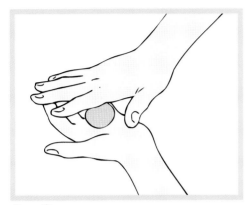

Step 2

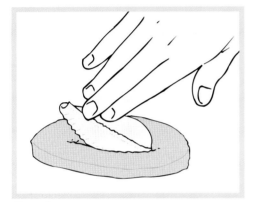

Step 3

Steps to follow

1 Cut a block of clay for each child. Make it large enough to make several fossils.

2 Pinch off a piece of clay. Roll the clay flat with a rolling pin or a roller to approximately 1.25 cm thick. It may be an irregular shape.

3 Place a shell or other object you want to imprint on top of the clay. Press down gently with your hand or with the roller.

4 Lift the object to see if the impression is deep enough.

5 Let the clay dry thoroughly and fire it in a kiln.

6 Instead of glazing the 'fossils', spray them with a fixative to preserve them. An adult should spray the projects in a well-ventilated area.

How to use a rolling pin or roller with clay

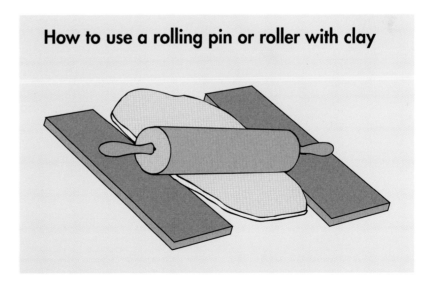

Making beads

Age range: 5–11 years

Create clay beads for use in making necklaces and costumes.

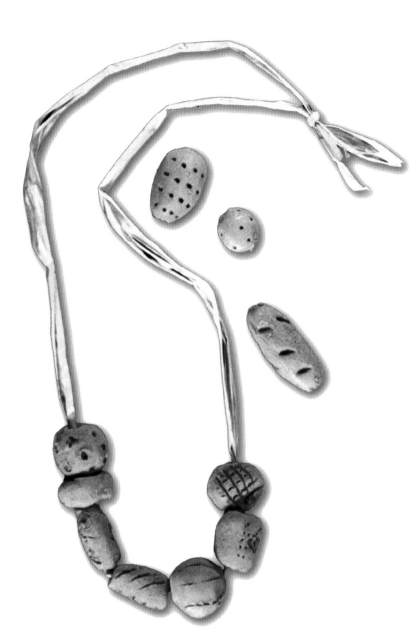

Vocabulary

glaze

texture

Materials

- clay
- newspaper
- cardboard with clean paper cover
- rolling pin
- toothpicks
- cords for stringing beads
- glazes or paints
- spray fixative (optional)
- access to a kiln

Project notes

- Set up a work area with newspaper and a suitable cardboard work surface.
- Clay shrinks while drying, so make sure the hole in each bead is large enough to fit the cord or string through.

Let's talk about it

- Describe the way clay feels in your hands. Does it feel cold, elastic, wet or dry?
- Why do you think people still like to sculpt with clay?
- How is sculpting with clay like painting a picture?

National Curriculum: Art & design
KS1: 2a, 2b, 4a, 4b, 5b, 5c
KS2: 2a, 2b, 2c, 4a, 4b, 5b, 5c
QCA Schemes of Work: Art & design
Unit 1C – What is sculpture?
Unit 6B – What a performance
Scottish 5-14 Guidelines: Art & design
Using materials, techniques, skills and media:
Using media; Using visual elements
Expressing feelings, ideas, thoughts
and solutions: Creating and designing.
Communicating

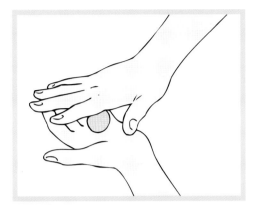

Step 2

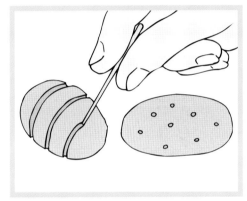

Step 3

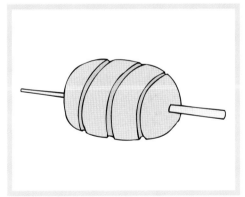

Step 4

Steps to follow

1 Cut a block of clay for each child. Make it large enough to make up to a dozen beads.

2 Pinch off small pieces of clay and roll them between the palms of the hands. Create the desired shape: round, oblong, oval or square.

3 Roll the piece over a textured cloth or use a toothpick to create a design. Keep the designs simple.

4 Make a hole through the bead with a toothpick. Allow for shrinkage of the clay as it dries.

5 Dry the beads and fire them.

Finishing touches

• Beads created from terracotta clay are attractive with only a spray fixative used as a sealer.

• If a glaze is used, be sure to elevate the beads in the kiln so they do not stick to the shelf.

• Finishing with tempera paint creates a primitive look, and the beads will wear well if sprayed with a fixative.

Pinch pots

Create pottery using a pinching and pulling method.

Vocabulary

paddling

pinching

pulling

Materials

- clay
- newspaper
- cardboard with clean paper cover
- cup of water
- sponge
- wooden spoon
- texturing tools: forks, shells, burlap
- access to a kiln

Project notes

- Model the process of making a pinch pot for the children before they begin. This will give you an opportunity to point out the techniques and possible pitfalls of the process.

- It is easy to weaken the walls of the pot by making them too thin. About 0.5 cm is a good thickness.

Let's talk about it

- Clay is very elastic. How does this help in making a pinch pot?

- What other things besides pots could be created with this method?

National Curriculum: Art & design
KS1: 2a, 2b, 4a, 4b, 5b, 5c
KS2: 2a, 2b, 2c, 4a, 4b, 5b, 5c
QCA Schemes of Work: Art & design
Unit 1C – What is sculpture?
Unit 5B – Containers
Scottish 5-14 Guidelines: Art & design
Using materials, techniques, skills and media:
Using media; Using visual elements
Expressing feelings, ideas, thoughts and solutions:
Creating and designing; Communicating

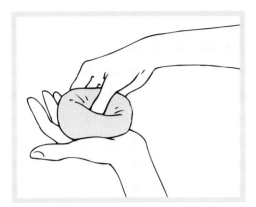

Step 2

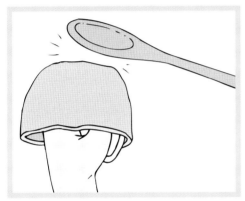

Step 3

Step 5

Steps to follow

1 Cut a piece of clay the size of a tennis ball for each child. Using hands and a flat surface, round the clay into a smooth ball shape.

2 Holding the ball in one palm, start pinching a pocket in the centre with the thumb and fingers of the other hand. Don't let the walls get too thin. Work the pot slowly by pinching and pulling.

3 Smooth away any fingerprints with a wooden spoon. Place the pot over one fist and gently slap it with the flat surface of the spoon. This process of smoothing out the lumps and fingerprints is called paddling.

4 The top edge of the pot will be irregular. You may trim it with a knife or leave it uneven to add character.

5 Stand the pot on a flat surface that is covered with clean paper. Gently press down to form the base. This will prevent the finished pot from rocking.

6 Add texture to pots with tools such as forks, shells, or burlap. Press into the outer walls to leave an impression. If cracks appear, use water and a sponge to smooth out the clay.

7 After the pot is completely dry, place it in a kiln to fire. Glaze and fire again. If glazes are not available, try painting with tempera and finishing with a spray fixative.

Coil pots

Vocabulary

scoring

slip

Materials

- clay
- newspaper
- cardboard with clean paper cover
- cup of water
- plastic knife
- texturing tools
- rolling pin
- slip (see page 86, tip 4)
- glaze (optional)
- craft stick
- smooth stone
- access to a kiln

Project notes

- Model the process of making a coil pot before the children begin. This is an opportunity to point out techniques and possible pitfalls of the process.

- If the pots are to be glazed and are designed to hold food, remember to use non-toxic glazes.

Let's talk about it

- How is the clay different when fired rather than air dried?

- How is a coil pot different from a pinch pot?

- Do we think about form and design while creating a pot as we do when painting a picture?

National Curriculum: Art & design
KS1: 2a, 2b, 4a, 4b, 5b, 5c
KS2: 2a, 2b, 2c, 4a, 4b, 5b, 5c
QCA Schemes of Work: Art & design
Unit 1C – What is sculpture?
Unit 5B – Containers
Scottish 5-14 Guidelines: Art & design
Using materials, techniques, skills and media:
Using media; Using visual elements
Expressing feelings, ideas, thoughts
and solutions: Creating and designing;
Communicating

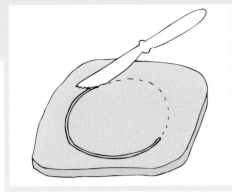

Step 2

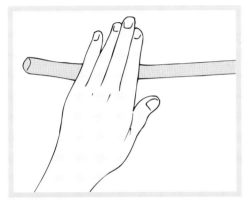

Step 3

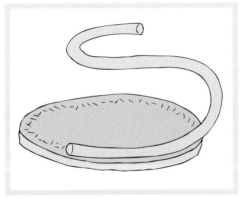

Step 4

Step 6

Steps to follow

1 Start with a block of clay the size of a tennis ball. Pinch off a piece the size of a golf ball to form the base of the pot. Flatten this piece of clay with a roller to 0.5 cm in thickness.

2 Decide on a shape for the base and cut out the shape with the plastic knife. Place it on the paper-covered cardboard. Use this paper to turn the clay while working.

3 Pinch off another golf ball-size piece of clay. Squeeze it into a rope. Roll it from the centre toward the ends until it is a coil about the width of a finger. If the clay becomes dry, add a bit of water.

4 Moisten the base, score the surface with the knife, and add a layer of slip. Lift the coil carefully so it doesn't stretch, and place it on the base. Use a craft stick in a wiping motion to make the coil adhere to the base permanently.

5 Continue to add coils on top of the first coil. With each new coil, the previous surface must be scored and layered with slip. To make the pot wider, place each new coil to the outside of the previous one. To make the walls contract, place each coil to the inside of the previous one.

6 After several coils are in place, support the outside wall with one hand and use a smooth stone dipped in water to smooth the inside. Then smooth the outside wall.

7 After all the coils are in place and the entire surface is smoothed, add decorations with texturing tools. Dry the pottery thoroughly and fire it. Glaze the pot (optional) and then fire it again.

Hanging slab vase

Create a vase starting with a flat piece or slab of clay.

Vocabulary

scoring

slip

Materials

- clay
- newspaper
- cardboard with clean paper cover
- cup of water
- plastic knife
- texturing tools such as nails, pencils and orange sticks
- sponge
- burlap or other textured fabric
- rolling pin
- slip
- access to a kiln

Project notes

- Model the process of making a slab pot before the children begin. This will give you an opportunity to point out techniques and possible pitfalls of the process.
- Moisten clay periodically with the sponge and water to prevent cracking.
- Fill the finished vase with dried flowers or leaves.

Let's talk about it

- How is making a slab pot different from making a pinch or coil pot?
- What types of materials from nature could be used to decorate the slab pot?

National Curriculum: Art & design
KS1: 2a, 2b, 4a, 4b, 5b, 5c
KS2: 2a, 2b, 2c, 4a, 4b, 5b, 5c
QCA Schemes of Work: Art & design
Unit 1C – What is sculpture?
Unit 5B – Containers
Scottish 5–14 Guidelines: Art & design
Using materials, techniques, skills and media:
Using media; Using visual elements
Expressing feelings, ideas, thoughts
and solutions: Creating and designing.
Communicating

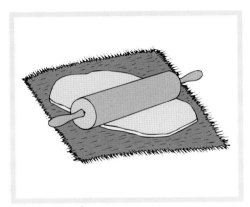

Steps 1 and 2

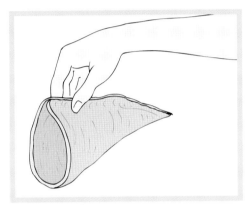

Steps 3 and 4

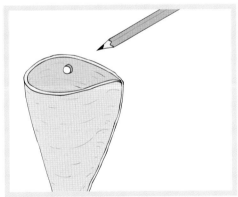

Step 5

Steps to follow

1 Cut a block of clay the size of a tennis ball. To prevent cracking, moisten the clay with a sponge and water before starting.

2 Place the clay on a piece of burlap or other fabric with a coarse texture. Use a rolling pin to flatten the clay to 0.5 cm thick. Leave the edges uneven or trim with a plastic knife.

3 Peel the clay from the fabric and roll it into the shape of a cornucopia. Be careful not to damage the texture.

4 With a knife, score the edges where the clay overlaps and add slip to act as glue. Gently press or pinch the edges together to seal.

5 Punch a hole with a pencil approximately 1.25 cm from the top so the pot can be hung from a wall.

6 Place the vase on a clean sheet of paper and let it dry completely. Fire the pot in the kiln.

7 Glaze the pot inside and out and fire it again.

Basic tiles

Learn to make a basic tile using a slab technique.

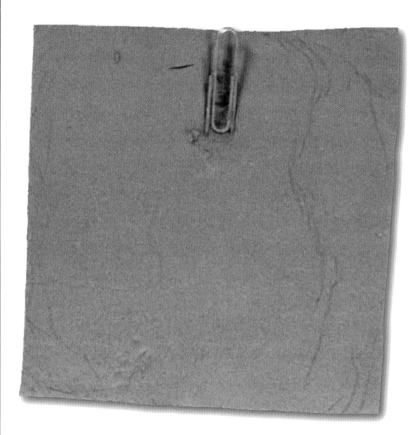

Vocabulary

texture

Materials

- clay
- newspaper
- cardboard with clean paper cover
- rolling pin
- paper clips (optional)
- plastic knife
- texturing tools
- 13 cm square templates made from cardboard
- glaze (optional)

Project notes

- Model the process of making a tile before the children begin. Use this time to refer to the tips listed on page 86. These reminders can make the difference between a successful project and a disaster.

- It is important to work on cardboard with a clean paper cover. This surface keeps the tile from sticking to the work area and allows the clay to be picked up without distorting the shape.

Let's talk about it

- What are some uses for clay tiles?
- Where might you see clay tiles in your home and community?
- How is making tiles similar to making slab pots?

National Curriculum: Art & design
KS1: 2a, 2b, 4a, 4b, 5b, 5c
KS2: 2a, 2b, 2c, 4a, 4b, 5b, 5c
QCA Schemes of Work: Art & design
Unit 1C – What is sculpture?
Unit 3B – Investigating pattern
Scottish 5–14 Guidelines: Art & design
Using materials, techniques, skills and media:
Using media; Using visual elements
Expressing feelings, ideas, thoughts
and solutions: Creating and designing;
Communicating

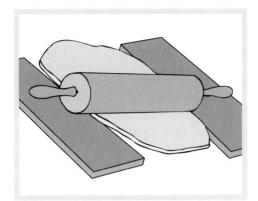

Step 1

Step 2

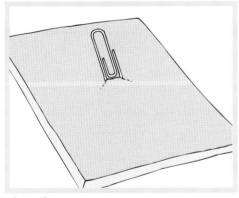

Step 3

Steps to follow

1 Cut a piece of clay. Place the clay on the cardboard covered with clean paper. Using the rolling pin, flatten the clay starting from the middle and working out toward the edges until the slab is about 0.5 cm thick.

2 Place the template on the clay and roll over it with the rolling pin to leave a slight impression. Use the knife to cut around the template edges. Remove the scraps and save them for future use. Remove the template. Now the basic clay tile has been created.

3 Insert a paper clip hanger if the tile is to be hung on the wall. Insert it toward the top of the tile at an angle with the loop sticking out. Be careful not to push it through the tile.

4 Pick up the paper the tile is on and flip it over, clip side down, onto a clean paper. Peel the paper off the tile.

5 Decorate the tile with texturing tools. Let it dry and fire it in the kiln. Children may choose to glaze the textured tile. Then the tile will have to be fired again.

Suggested texturing techniques:

- cross-hatching with a fork
- impressions of leaves or feathers
- impressions of pasta letter forms to create words
- pictures drawn with toothpicks

Nature tiles

Age range: 5–11 years

Create a textured tile using the slab technique and items collected from nature.

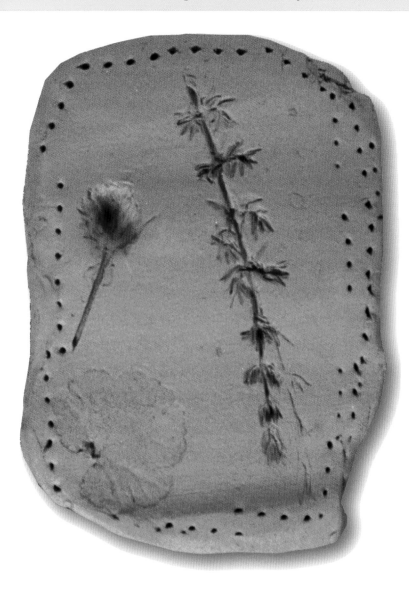

Vocabulary

impression

printing

Materials

- clay
- newspaper
- cardboard with clean paper cover
- rolling pin
- plastic knife
- templates made from cardboard
- fresh flowers, leaves, etc.
- paper clips
- tempera paints (optional)
- spray fixative (optional)
- access to a kiln

Project notes

- Before beginning the project, review the procedure for making a basic tile on page 72 and the tips on page 86.

- Do this as part of a science lesson. Children can collect their own materials for imprinting tiles.

- This tile is good to use as a coaster or trivet. It would make a nice gift.

- Do not glaze these tiles – it will ruin the impressions. Instead, paint with tempera paint and spray with a fixative.

Let's talk about it

- How is imprinting in clay similar to printing with paint on paper? How is it different?

- Can you see and feel how the texture of the clay changes when the objects are imprinted?

National Curriculum: Art & design
KS1: 2a, 2b, 4a, 4b, 5b, 5c
KS2: 2a, 2b, 2c, 4a, 4b, 5b, 5c
QCA Schemes of Work: Art & design
Unit 1C – What is sculpture?
Unit 3B – Investigating pattern
Scottish 5–14 Guidelines: Art & design
Using materials, techniques, skills and media:
Investigating visually and recording; Using media;
Using visual elements
Expressing feelings, ideas, thoughts and solutions:
Creating and designing; Communicating

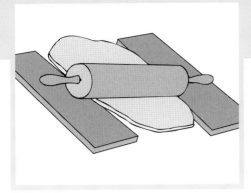

Step 1

Step 1

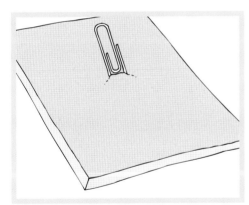

Step 2

Step 4

Steps to follow

1 Start by making a basic tile (see page 72 for details). Roll out a chunk of clay. Choose a template shape and place it on the clay. Gently roll over it to leave an impression on the clay. Then cut out the shape with a plastic knife.

2 Insert a paper clip toward the top edge of the tile if it is to be hung up. Flip the tile over.

3 Choose a fresh flower or leaf to imprint. Make sure it has good detail so the imprint will not disappear when the clay dries.

4 Place the object or objects on the tile and gently but firmly press with the rolling pin. Be sure to get a clear impression before removing the objects.

5 Gently remove the objects from the clay impression. Set the tiles aside to dry.

6 Fire the tiles in the kiln.

7 Tiles may be left in their natural state or painted with tempera paint. If painted, spray the tiles with fixative.

Picture frame tiles

Create a frame from a slab of clay. Add a textured design using a variety of tools.

Vocabulary

texture

Materials

- clay
- newspaper
- cardboard with clean paper cover
- rolling pin
- plastic knife
- templates cut from cardboard
- paper clips
- small photos
- glue
- texturing tools such as pencils, craft sticks, nails and toothpicks
- tempera paints (optional)
- spray fixative (optional)
- access to a kiln

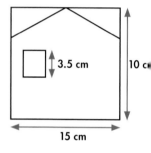

Project notes

- Review the steps for making a tile plus the helpful tips on page 86.
- Glazing these projects tends to obscure the textured design. Tempera paint and fixative may be a wiser choice for decoration.

Let's talk about it

- How does crafting with clay resemble weaving?
- How are printing and clay crafting similar and how are they different?

National Curriculum: Art & design
KS1: 2a, 2b, 4a, 4b, 5b, 5c
KS2: 2a, 2b, 2c, 4a, 4b, 5b, 5c

QCA Schemes of Work: Art & design
Unit 1C – What is sculpture?
Unit 2C – Can buildings speak?

Scottish 5-14 Guidelines: Art & design
Using materials, techniques, skills and media:
Using media; Using visual elements
Expressing feelings, ideas, thoughts
and solutions: Creating and designing;
Communicating

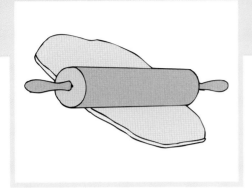

Step 1

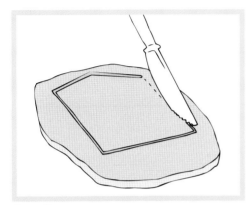

Step 2

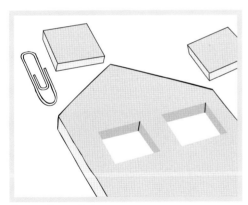

Steps 3 and 4

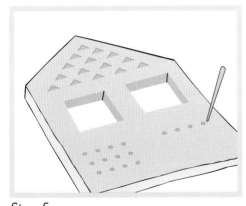

Step 5

Steps to follow

1 Make a basic tile. Place a chunk of clay on the cardboard. Using the rolling pin, flatten the clay starting from the middle and working out toward the edges until the slab is about 0.5 cm thick.

2 Choose a template such as a rectangle or square for the shape of the frame – perhaps the shape of a house. Place the template over the tile and make an imprint using the rolling pin. Cut away scraps and save for later use.

3 Cut a rectangular template for the inside of the frame. Make an imprint of this template on the clay with the rolling pin. Cut out the rectangles with the plastic knife and remove them.

4 Insert a paper clip hanger if the tile is to be hung on the wall. Insert it toward the top at an angle with the loop sticking out. Be careful not to push it through the tile. Flip the tile over.

5 Using texturing tools, add designs to the frame. Items such as craft sticks, toothpicks and shells can be used to make wonderful textures.

6 Dry the tile thoroughly and fire it. If desired, add colour with tempera paint and spray with a fixative. These frames are also very effective left with the natural finish.

7 When the frame is finished, attach the pictures to the back of the frame with glue.

Whales

Create an animal sculpture using the basic pull-out method of sculpting.

Vocabulary

glaze

sculpture

Materials

- clay
- newspaper
- cardboard with clean paper cover
- cup of water
- craft stick
- toothpick
- access to a kiln

Project notes

- Experiment to see what kind of effects can be created with clay before doing a finished sculpture. Do not use the experimental clay to do the finished project. Air will have been trapped in the clay, which will cause problems during firing.

Origins of clay

Building with clay predates recorded history. Pottery and clay sculptures can be found in cultures throughout the world.

Let's talk about it

- What kinds of materials other than clay can be used for sculptures?
- How did pulling the tail of the whale up or down suggest movement?
- How do you think sculpting animals with clay started?

National Curriculum: Art & design
KS1: 2a, 2b, 4a, 4b, 5b, 5c
KS2: 2a, 2b, 2c, 4a, 4b, 5b, 5c

QCA Schemes of Work: Art & design
Unit 1C – What is sculpture?
Unit 5A – Objects and meanings

Scottish 5–14 Guidelines: Art & design
Using materials, techniques, skills and media:
Using media; Using visual elements
Expressing feelings, ideas, thoughts
and solutions: Creating and designing;
Communicating

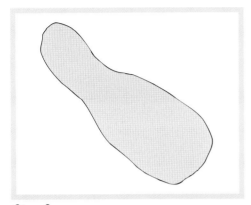

Step 2

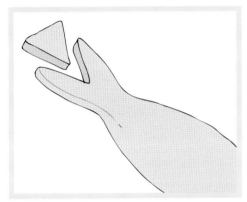

Step 3

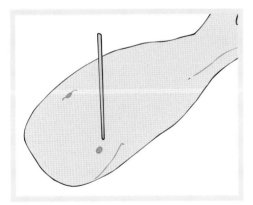

Step 4

Steps to follow

1 Cut clay to the size of a child's fist. Gently roll and mould the clay until it looks somewhat like a potato.

2 About a third of the way from the end of the clay 'potato', pull out a tail portion by gently squeezing your fingers around the piece of clay. Leave the majority of the clay for the head and body of the whale.

3 Flatten the tail area with your fingers. Don't make it too thin. Use a craft stick to cut V-shaped flukes at the end of the tail. You may want to pull out fins on both sides of the body.

4 Make eyes and a blow hole by gently pushing a toothpick in and out. Use the same toothpick to carve out a mouth. Also carve the artist's initials on the bottom.

5 At this point you can suggest movement by bending the tail up or down.

6 Poke two holes with a pencil in the underside of the thickest part of the whale body to aid the drying process. Dry the whale thoroughly and then fire it in a kiln.

7 Adding a glaze makes the whale look shiny and wet. Fire again after glazing.

Bears

Create a more sophisticated animal sculpture using a basic pull-out method of sculpting.

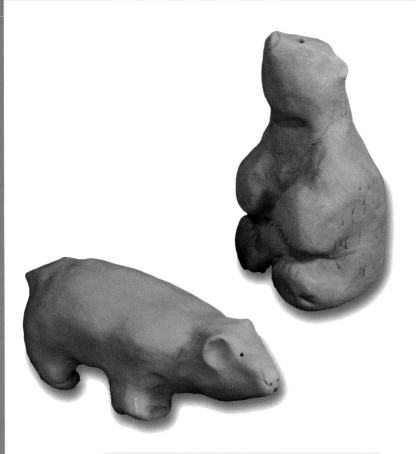

Vocabulary

pull-out method

Materials

- clay
- newspaper
- cardboard with clean paper cover
- craft stick
- toothpick
- cup of water
- plastic fork or comb
- access to a kiln

Project notes

- As the bear is being sculpted, remember that it needs to stand up on four legs. However, if the bear is 'unsteady' on its feet, you can always have it sit down.

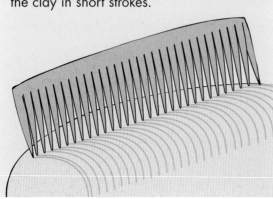

Create the bear's coarse fur by combing the clay in short strokes.

Let's talk about it

- Why is balance important when doing a sculpture?
- How did you create texture in your sculpture?

National Curriculum: Art & design
KS1: 2a, 2b, 4a, 4b, 5b, 5c
KS2: 2a, 2b, 2c, 4a, 4b, 5b, 5c

QCA Schemes of Work: Art & design
Unit 1C – What is sculpture?
Unit 5A – Objects and meanings

Scottish 5–14 Guidelines: Art & design
Using materials, techniques, skills and media:
Using media; Using visual elements
Expressing feelings, ideas, thoughts and solutions:
Creating and designing; Communicating

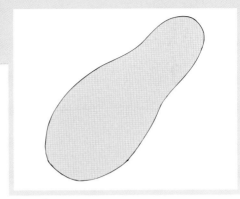

Step 1

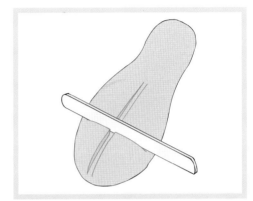

Step 2

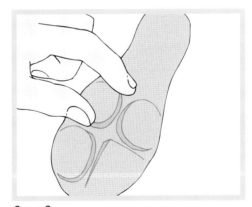

Step 3

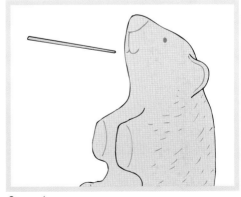

Step 4

Steps to follow

1 Cut the clay to about the size of an orange. Roll and pat the clay into a potato shape. Using about a third of the potato shape, gently pull out a head portion. Do not squeeze too hard. Bears have thick necks.

2 Turn the bear over on its back. Using a craft stick, mark lines for the legs.

3 Form the leg sections by gently pulling and pushing the clay into rounded legs. Keep the legs short and thick. Bears do not have long, thin legs.

4 Look at the head portion. Form the nose so it is slightly pointed. Use your thumb and forefinger to gently pinch out two ears. They should be rounded, set apart and not too thin. Use a toothpick to make eyes. Draw a line around the nose for definition.

5 Use a fork or comb to create texture for the fur by combing the clay with short strokes. Decide whether your bear will stand on all fours, sit down or lie down.

6 Poke two holes in the underside of the bear with a pencil to aid in drying. Fire the sculpture in the kiln.

7 Glazing is optional. If you are using a terracotta clay, the final product is very attractive without glaze.

Fantasy fish

Age range: 5–11 years

Create a fantasy fish sculpture while learning the add-on method of sculpting.

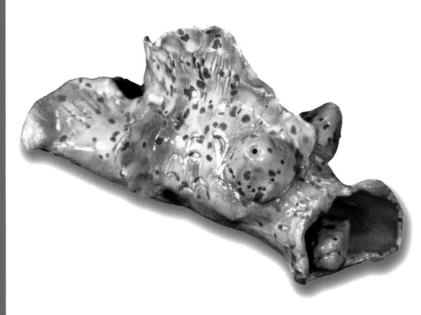

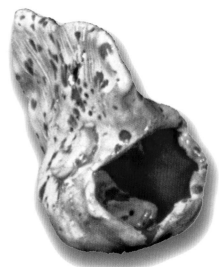

Vocabulary

add-on method

kiln

scoring

slip

Materials

- clay
- newspaper
- cardboard with clean paper cover
- rolling pin
- cup of water
- cup of slip (see page 86, tip 4)
- plastic knife
- texturing tools
- toothpicks
- small pieces of crumpled newspaper
- access to a kiln

Project notes

- Because this clay will be rolled out (eliminating air pockets), leftover clay may be used.
- If fish are to be used as ornaments for your aquarium, be sure to use non-toxic glazes.

Let's talk about it

- How is the add-on method of sculpting different from the pull-out method?
- How can using paper help in creating different effects in sculpting?

National Curriculum: Art & design
KS1: 2a, 2b, 4a, 4b, 5b, 5c
KS2: 2a, 2b, 2c, 4a, 4b, 5b, 5c
QCA Schemes of Work: Art & design
Unit 1C – What is sculpture?
Scottish 5–14 Guidelines: Art & design
Using materials, techniques, skills and media:
Using media; Using visual elements
Expressing feelings, ideas, thoughts and solutions:
Creating and designing; Communicating

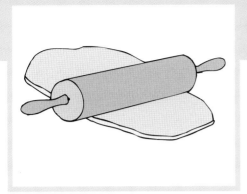

Step 1

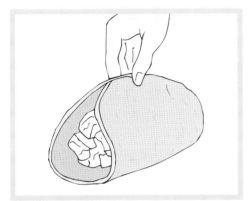

Steps 2 and 3

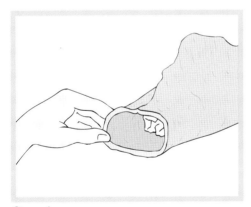

Step 4

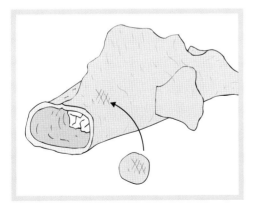

Step 5

Steps to follow

1 Start with a piece of clay about the size of an orange. Use a rolling pin to flatten the clay. Start rolling out from the middle until it is about 1.25 cm to 0.5 cm thick. Edges should not be uniform.

2 Place a tightly crumpled piece of newspaper in the centre of the clay slab. This will act as a form for the body of the fish.

3 Score the edges of the clay slab with a knife and add slip for glue. Pull up the two sides of the clay and pinch it together. This forms the top back of the fish.

4 Pinch the tail area together at one end. Pull and pinch the other end to form the head and open mouth. Don't worry about trapping the newspaper inside the fish. It will burn up when the clay is fired.

5 Create eyes by rolling small balls of clay in the palms. Score the back of the eyes and the eye area on the fish head. Using slip for glue, firmly set the eyes in place. Fins may also be added using the same procedure.

6 Allow the fish to dry thoroughly and then fire in the kiln.

7 Paint these fish with brightly coloured glazes and fire again.

Making faces

Age range: 5–11 years

Create a basic clay mask using slab, pull-out, and add-on techniques.

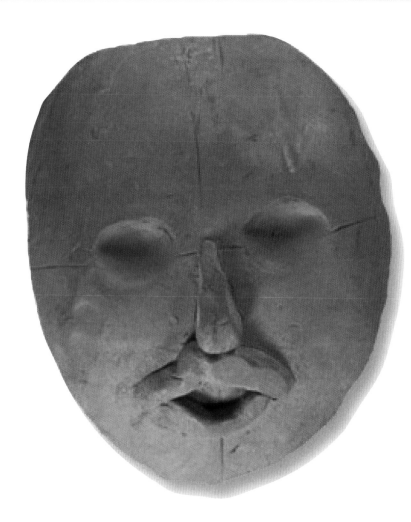

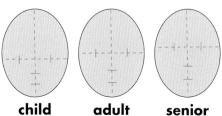

child   **adult**   **senior**

Vocabulary

add-on method   mould

pull-out method

Materials

- clay
- crumpled newspaper
- cardboard with clean paper cover
- plastic spoon
- cup of slip
- cup of water
- pencil
- rolling pin
- access to a kiln

Project notes

How to create features on a face:

- Draw a vertical line down the centre of the face.
- Draw a horizontal line across the face to mark the level of the eyes.
- Mark the centre of the eyes at about one-third the distance between the centre and sides of the face.
- Put the nose halfway between the eyes and mouth.
- Put the mouth between the nose and chin.

Let's talk about it

- Name all the different methods of clay crafting used in this project.
- How did you show feeling when developing the mouth and eyes?

National Curriculum: Art & design
KS1: 2a, 2b, 4a, 4b, 5b, 5c
KS2: 2a, 2b, 2c, 4a, 4b, 5b, 5c
QCA Schemes of Work: Art & design
Unit 1C – What is sculpture?
Unit 3A – Portraying relationships
Scottish 5–14 Guidelines: Art & design
Using materials, techniques, skills and media:
Investigating visually and recording; Using media; Using visual elements
Expressing feelings, ideas, thoughts and solutions: Creating and designing; Communicating

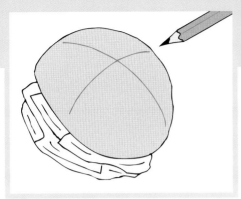

Steps 1 and 2

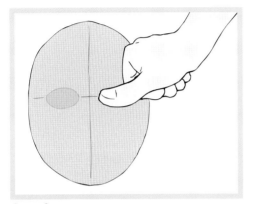

Step 3

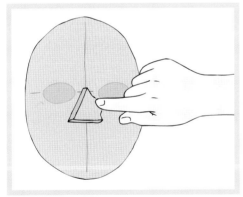

Step 4

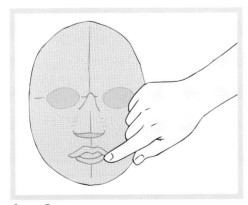

Step 5

Steps to follow

1 Start with a slab of clay about the size of an orange. Cut approximately 1.25 cm off the slab and set aside. This extra piece will be used to add facial features. Use your hands to carefully round the corners and flatten to an oval shape. The clay should be about 1.25 cm thick. Trim the edges of the oval to make it even.

2 Place the slab over crumpled newspaper. This will act as a mould. Ease the clay into a convex shape. If you want to hang the mask, make two holes in the top half, a finger width away from each side. Use a pencil to lightly draw placement lines on the face (see notes on page 84).

3 Use a spoon or your thumb to shape the eyes. Gently press in the eye shape on each side, being careful to make them even.

4 To make the nose, select a piece of the clay you set aside, and cut a pyramid shape with your knife. Score, apply slip to the edges, and join to the face. Smooth out the line around the nose with water. Shape the nose the way you like, using the pull-out method.

5 To make lips, roll a clay coil and attach it to the mouth area by scoring and using slip. Shape the mouth into a smile or a frown.

6 If desired, give the mask character by adding eyeballs, hair, eyebrows or whiskers.

7 Dry the mask thoroughly on the mould. Then remove the mould and fire the mask. If you glaze the mask, fire it once again.

Ten tips for using clay

1 Have all the materials ready before starting. Suddenly remembering you need to put on an apron is unsettling once your hands are covered with clay!

2 Check clay for air bubbles. Air pockets can expand in the kiln and spoil children's artwork. If air bubbles are present, wedge the clay for at least five minutes. Wedge by using the palm of your hands to lightly press down, much like kneading bread. Never poke fingers into the clay or flatten and fold it over. This is a sure way to cause air bubbles.

3 Try using a rolling pin or a dowel rod (roller) to roll out clay. To ensure uniform thickness, place two boards of the desired thickness on either side of the clay before rolling it out.

4 Make slip before starting a project that requires pieces to be attached. Slip is clay dissolved in water to the consistency of cake batter. Never use plain water to attach pieces. Slip acts like glue to hold layers of clay together.

5 Use water to moisten clay if cracking occurs. Be careful not to use too much, as it will take longer for the pottery to dry.

6 Use a sponge dipped in water to smooth lumps and cracking.

7 Place cardboard covered with a piece of clean paper (not newspaper) on the work surface. When the project is finished, you can peel the paper off easily. If you work directly on the cardboard, your project may stick to it. The cardboard acts as a tray when the pottery needs to be moved.

8 When you attach pieces to each other, always score both parts and use slip.

9 Always make sure the piece is completely dry before putting it in the kiln. If it is cold to the touch, it still has moisture in it and will blow up if fired. The piece will feel warm when completely dry.

10 If a project is to hold food that is not wrapped, such as soup or a drink, check the glazes to make sure that they are non-toxic and have no lead.

Creative Activities • Art and Design Projects • **www.scholastic.co.uk**

Recyclables

This chapter highlights how everyday objects and rubbish can be turned into different and interesting objects by using a variety of simple art and craft techniques. By learning the skills of these techniques, children can experiment and create their own unique gifts or useable objects.

The projects in this chapter use a wide range of craft skills and techniques including papier-mâché, collage, book binding, three-dimensional paper folding, candle making, quilt designing, Japanese paper folding and tin smithing.

The recycled materials used include old trays, plastic bottle, tin foil plates, old magazines and comics, paper, old wax crayons and wallpaper.

Recycling objects into something special is a very satisfying process. By learning the skills of basic crafts, the children can see beyond the old objects and start to think of ways they can create beautiful objects in an inexpensive way.

Contents

Papier-mâché trays

Age range: 5–11 years

Create a decorative tray using recycled materials while learning the art of papier-mâché.

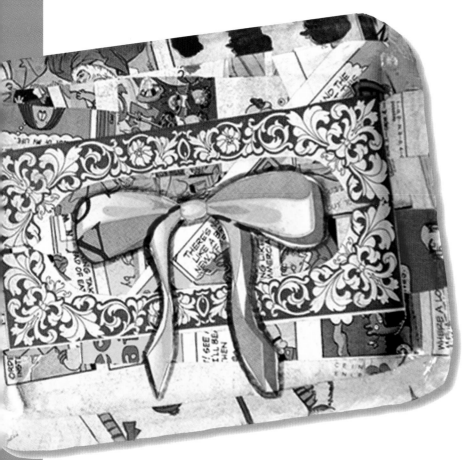

Vocabulary

papier-mâché

Materials

- foam trays (any colour or size)
- magazines
- newspapers (torn or cut into strips)
- water
- scissors
- bowls for mixture
- papier-mâché mixture
- varnish
- white glue
- paintbrush

Project notes

- Wash all foam trays in soapy water and dry them before starting.
- Set up a work area and ask the children wear smocks.
- The children should dip each piece of paper in the papier-mâché mixture rather than placing the paper strips into the mixture all at once. This keeps the paper from breaking down too much.
- The varnish should be applied in a well-ventilated area by an adult.

Let's talk about it

- What is papier-mâché?
- What does papier-mâché mean?
- Why is papier-mâché considered a form of sculpture?

National Curriculum: Art & design
KS1: 2a, 2b, 4a, 4b, 5b, 5c
KS2: 2a, 2b, 2c, 4a, 4b, 5b, 5c

QCA Schemes of Work: Art & design
Unit 1B – Investigating materials
Unit 5B – Containers

Scottish 5-14 Guidelines: Art & design
Using materials, techniques, skills and media:
Using media; Using visual elements
Expressing feelings, ideas, thoughts and solutions: Creating and designing;
Communicating

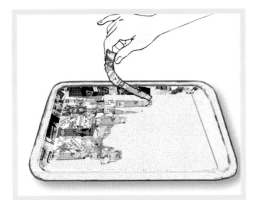

Steps 1 and 2

Step 3

Step 5

Steps to follow

1 Tear newspapers into strips. Make the papier-mâché mixture in bowls or buckets.

2 Dip each strip of paper in the papier-mâché mixture. Smooth the excess glue from the strip of paper before placing it on the tray. Too much glue will result in long drying times.

3 Smooth and overlap each piece of paper so that the ends are tidy. Follow the form of the tray. After one side of the tray is covered, let it dry.

4 Proceed to the other side of the tray. Overlap each piece of paper until the surface is covered. Let it dry throughly.

5 Cut colourful pictures from magazines. Dip these pictures in the papier-mâché mixture and smooth them onto the front of the tray. Let the tray dry. Then cover the back of the tray with pictures.

6 When the tray is completely dry, protect the surface by brushing on a coat of white glue.

Papier-mâché can be created from different kinds of mixtures

Method 1 – Use one part glue to two parts water and mix well.

Method 2 – Use wallpaper paste mixed according to package directions.

Collage containers

Age range: 5–11 years

Create a pot or bowl from a discarded plastic jug while learning about collage.

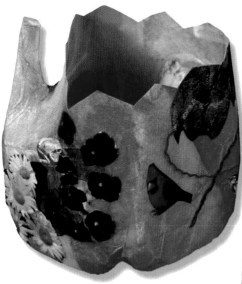

Vocabulary

collage

design

Materials

- plastic milk or detergent bottles
- scissors
- glue – equal parts white glue and water
- bowls (for glue mixture)
- paintbrush
- strings
- magazine pictures
- tissue or wrapping paper
- spray varnish (optional)

Project notes

- Use small pictures from magazines to decorate the jugs. Pictures of flowers, birds or small animals fit the theme of this project.
- Ask the children to wear smocks and work in a designated area, as this project can be messy.

Let's talk about it

- Compare the techniques of collage and papier-mâché.
- What kinds of materials might be used in making a collage?
- Why is it important to overlap materials when doing collage?

National Curriculum: Art & design
KS1: 2a, 2b, 4a, 4b, 5b, 5c
KS2: 2a, 2b, 2c, 4a, 4b, 5b, 5c
QCA Schemes of Work: Art & design
Unit 1B – Investigating materials
Unit 5B – Containers
Scottish 5–14 Guidelines: Art & design
Using materials, techniques, skills and media:
Using media; Using visual elements
Expressing feelings, ideas, thoughts and solutions:
Creating and designing; Communicating

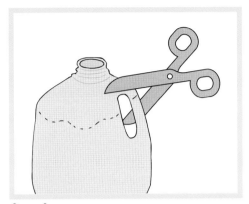

Step 1

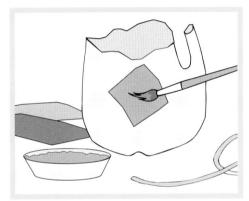

Steps 2 and 3

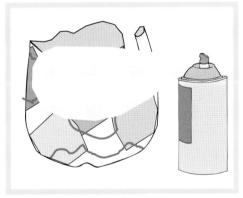

Step 5

Steps to follow

1 Wash a discarded plastic bottle or jug and dry it. Cut off the top and make it the desired size.

2 Cut up the tissue or wrapping paper into small pieces. Brush glue on the surface of the jug. Lay the paper pieces on the glued surface and brush glue over them. Let this layer dry completely.

3 Cut pictures from discarded magazines or junk mail. Collect bits of string to add to the collage.

4 Add the pictures and other items to the jug, using the glue mixture and the brush. Make sure all edges are glued securely. Develop a pleasing design by overlapping the pictures and glueing them in place. The key to good collage is overlapping the paper edges carefully.

5 When the collage is complete, set the jug aside to dry overnight. Then spray on varnish, if desired.

What is collage?

Collage is an art technique that uses a variety of papers and fabrics to create a design or picture. The various pieces are glued together onto a background of paper or cardboard or other objects.

Scrapbooks

Age range: 5–11 years

Create a scrapbook using recycled newspapers while learning a basic form of bookbinding.

Vocabulary

bookbinding

Materials

- thick cardboard
- newspapers or comics
- white glue mixed with a small amount of water
- paintbrush
- ruler
- pencil
- paper cutter or heavy-duty scissors
- a hole punch
- wool or shoelaces

Project notes

- A paper cutter is helpful for cutting the cardboard.
- Use this scrapbook as a class journal or as a folder in which children collect class work they want to save and share.

Let's talk about it

- What other materials might be used to create a covering for a book or folder?
- Discuss the different ways the tie binding may be wrapped.

National Curriculum: Art & design
KS1: 2a, 2b, 4a, 4b, 5b, 5c
KS2: 2a, 2b, 2c, 4a, 4b, 5b, 5c

QCA Schemes of Work: Art & design
Unit 1B – Investigating materials

Scottish 5–14 Guidelines: Art & design
Using materials, techniques, skills and media:
Using media; Using visual elements
Expressing feelings, ideas, thoughts and solutions:
Creating and designing; Communicating

Steps 1 and 2

Step 4

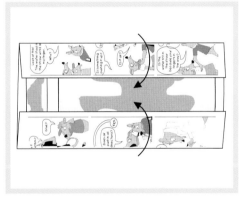

Step 5

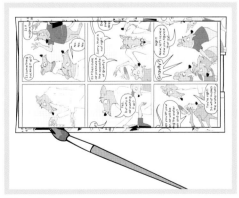

Step 6

Steps to follow

1 Cut the cardboard to the desired size using a ruler to measure. Cut off a 5 cm section of each piece of cardboard. This small section will act as a hinge when the two pieces are joined with the newspaper.

2 Choose sheets from the newspaper or comic with interesting print. Cut two rectangles that are larger than the cardboard. Lay them out on a large surface.

3 Place the cardboard pieces in the centre of the newspaper sheet. Draw around each piece of cardboard with a pencil.

4 Remove the cardboard. Place the cardboard on a flat surface and brush one side of it with the glue and water mixture. Place the cardboard glue-side down back on the newspaper in the area designated by the pencil outlines.

5 Brush glue around the edges of the cardboard. Fold the newspaper border over and press it into the glue.

6 Cut newspaper sheets for the endpapers (inside covering). Brush glue on the inside of the cardboard and lay the newspaper in place over it.

7 When both covers are complete and the glue is dry, punch holes in the left-hand margins and use shoelaces or wool to hold the book together.

Window hangings

Age range: 5–11 years

Practise tin-smithing techniques while making a decorative hanging.

Vocabulary

folk art

stencil

tin smithing

Materials

- tinfoil plates
- nails
- a hammer or a block of wood
- thick cardboard remnants
- folk art patterns or stencils
- pencil and paper
- string

Project notes

- Safety should be emphasized in this project because children are working with hammers and nails.

- Foil plates are best. Children will have an easier time tracing the pattern onto the plate and minimal effort is needed to punch the design with the nail. Work on pieces of cardboard to avoid damaging the table or floor surface.

Let's talk about it

- How is tin smithing different from other art forms such as carving or weaving?
- What kinds of objects would a tin smith make?

National Curriculum: Art & design
KS1: 2a, 2b, 4a, 4b, 5b, 5c
KS2: 2a, 2b, 2c, 4a, 4b, 5b, 5c
QCA Schemes of Work: Art & design
Unit 1B – Investigating materials
Scottish 5–14 Guidelines: Art & design
Using materials, techniques, skills and media:
Using media; Using visual elements
Expressing feelings, ideas, thoughts and solutions:
Creating and designing; Communicating

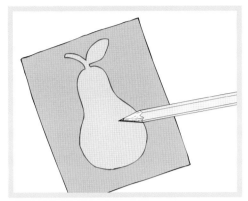

Step 1

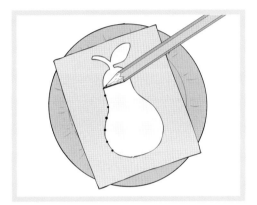

Step 2

Step 3

Steps to follow

1 Trace a simple pattern onto paper to serve as a stencil.

2 Place the pattern on the inside flat surface of the foil plate. Trace the pattern with a pencil, making slight indentations in the soft foil. Remove the pattern.

3 Put the plate on a piece of thick cardboard. Using a nail and a hammer, punch holes following the pattern lines. Only a tap is needed to punch the hole. Keep the holes at least 0.5 cm but not more than 1.25 cm apart.

4 Hold the finished piece to the light to check for areas that may need extra holes.

5 Punch a hole for a string loop. Hang the project in a window and let the light stream through.

Typical folk art designs

3-D paper decorations

Use paper-folding techniques to create a three-dimensional decoration from old magazines.

Vocabulary

three-dimensional

Materials

- magazines
- spray paints (various colours)
- string
- stapler

Project notes

- Create different patterns by changing the folds:
  - fold pages twice instead of once
  - fold half the pages, then flip the magazine around and continue folding to create an interesting twisted pattern
- Let the children experiment with different folds to discover the effects they can create.
- A light layer of gold or silver spray paint gives a gilded look.

Let's talk about it

- How was dimension created in this project?
- In what ways can this be used besides as a decoration?
- What is the art of Japanese paper folding called? (Origami.)

National Curriculum: Art & design
KS1: 2a, 2b, 4a, 4b, 5b, 5c
KS2: 2a, 2b, 2c, 4a, 4b, 5b, 5c
QCA Schemes of Work: Art & design
Unit 1B – Investigating materials
Scottish 5–14 Guidelines: Art & design
Using materials, techniques, skills and media:
Using media; Using visual elements
Expressing feelings, ideas, thoughts and solutions:
Creating and designing; Communicating

Step 1

Step 2

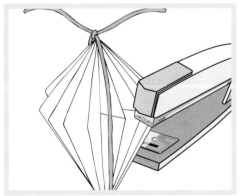

Step 3

Steps to follow

1 Give each child a magazine. Start by folding each page from the top right corner to the centre spine of the magazine. Then fold the bottom corner into the spine. Crease the folds firmly. Continue in this manner until all pages are folded.

2 Once the pages are folded, loop the string through the centre of the magazine and tie it, leaving enough string to hang the decoration.

3 Bend the front cover around to meet the back cover, creating a three-dimensional shape. Staple the covers together. (If the magazine is very thin, fold two magazines and staple them together.)

4 Spray the decoration with several colours of paint. An adult should do the spraying in a well-ventilated area.

5 Hang the decoration to dry.

Designer soap boxes

Age range: 5–11 years

Learn about camouflage while creating a storage container from reusable detergent boxes.

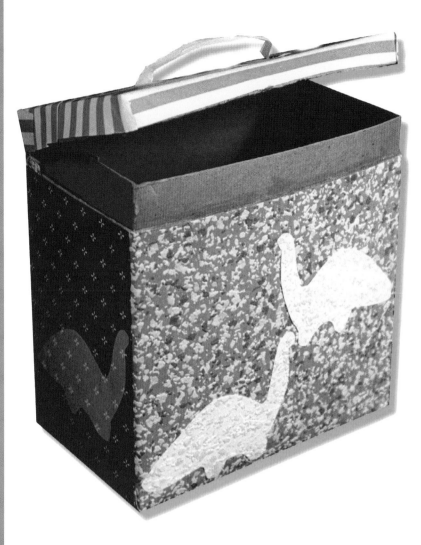

Vocabulary

camouflage

optical illusion

Materials

- empty washing powder boxes with lids
- wallpaper remnants (in contrasting colours)
- biscuit cutters or stencils
- pencil
- scissors
- glue, diluted with water
- paintbrush
- newspapers

Project notes

- Plan ahead and ask local wallpaper stores to save out-of-date sample books for you. Most paper patterns in the books will have the same pattern repeated in different colour choices. These are perfect for this project.

Let's talk about it

- How is camouflage used in nature?
- How is camouflage used by humans?
- Can you think of ways camouflage has been used in art?

National Curriculum: Art & design
KS1: 2a, 2b, 4a, 4b, 5b, 5c
KS2: 2a, 2b, 2c, 4a, 4b, 5b, 5c
QCA Schemes of Work: Art & design
Unit 1B – Investigating materials
Unit 5B – Containers
Scottish 5-14 Guidelines: Art & design
Using materials, techniques, skills and media:
Using media; Using visual elements
Expressing feelings, ideas, thoughts and solutions:
Creating and designing; Communicating.

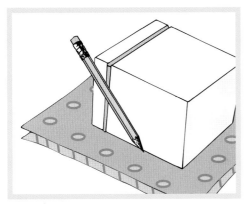

Step 2

Step 3

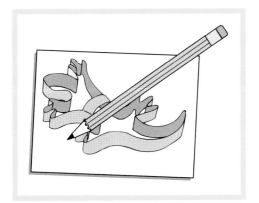

Step 4

Steps to follow

1 Choose wallpaper remnants with the same or a similar pattern, but in different colours. Plan which paper will go on each side of the box and lid.

2 Lay the box on the wallpaper pieces and trace around the edges with a pencil. Cut out the pieces.

3 Lay the cut pieces of wallpaper facedown on sheets of newspaper. Brush on the glue. Place the glued paper on the box. Cover the entire surface.

4 Use a pencil to trace around the stencils or biscuit cutters on the extra pieces of wallpaper. Cut out the images and glue them to the box. If using striped papers, try to match them in a way that 'hides' the shape most effectively.

5 Allow the box to dry and use the 'designer' box for storage.

The designs in this project are built with images laid on top of a background. The goal is to create these shapes from another paper that blends subtly into the background design.

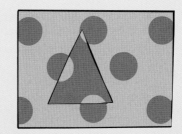

Crayon candles

Age range: 7–11 years

Learn candle making while using reusable products.

Vocabulary

candlewick   mould

paraffin

Materials

- broken crayons (with paper removed)
- wax (paraffin)
- wick or string
- thermometer
- double boiler
- moulds (such as milk cartons, yoghurt cups, cans)
- colour wheel (see page 23)
- vegetable oil
- heat source
- newspapers

Project notes

- Always use caution when working with hot wax. Never melt wax directly on a heat source – always use a double boiler. The boiling water will keep the wax from burning. Melting and pouring of hot wax should be done by an adult.

- Work over newspapers for easy clean-up.

- Two-colour layered candles can be made by pouring one colour, letting it set, and then pouring the other colour.

National Curriculum: Art & design
KS1: 2a, 2b, 4a, 4b, 5b, 5c
KS2: 2a, 2b, 2c, 4a, 4b, 5b, 5c
QCA Schemes of Work: Art & design
Unit 1B – Investigating materials
Scottish 5–14 Guidelines: Art & design
Using materials, techniques, skills and media:
Using media; Using visual elements
Expressing feelings, ideas, thoughts and solutions:
Creating and designing; Communicating.

Let's talk about it

- Discuss how and why candles were first used.
- Look at different types of candles. How are they alike and different?
- Some candles are made of beeswax. What texture do these candles have?

Steps 2 and 3

Step 4

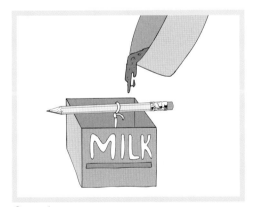

Step 6

Steps to follow

1 Look at a colour wheel to sort crayons into mixable colour piles. To make a green candle, add green crayons to the wax or mix blue and yellow crayons in the wax to make green.

2 Make sure the moulds are clean. Lightly coat the inside with cooking oil for easier removal of the finished candle.

3 Poke a tiny hole in the bottom of the mould for adding the wick. Thread a wick or string through the hole and tie a knot on the outside of the mould (Alternatively, use metal wick bases found in craft stores – these clamp onto the wick and sit in the base of the mould.)

4 To guarantee a straight wick in the candle, tie the top of the wick to a pencil. Rest the pencil across the top of the mould.

5 Break the paraffin into pieces and put in the top of a double boiler along with a thermometer. Heat the wax. When the wax reaches approximately 80° Celsius, add the crayons. Use the equivalent of three crayons per cup of wax.

6 When the crayons have melted, carefully pour the mixture into the moulds.

7 Let the candle set for at least three hours before removing it. Paper moulds such as milk cartons can be simply torn away.

Junk frames

Vocabulary

design

free form

three-dimensional

Materials

- two pieces of cardboard the same size
- white paste or glue with applicator
- found objects such as straws, bottle tops, can tabs and string
- scissors
- masking tape

Project notes

- Use leftover cardboard from writing pads and cereal boxes. Collect and share pieces of different sizes, shapes, and colours.

Let's talk about it

- How does working with three-dimensional objects add new challenges to creating a design?
- What kinds of theme frames might be created to complement certain photos or works of art?

National Curriculum: Art & design
KS1: 2a, 2b, 4a, 4b, 5b, 5c
KS2: 2a, 2b, 2c, 4a, 4b, 5b, 5c
QCA Schemes of Work: Art & design
Unit 1B – Investigating materials
Scottish 5–14 Guidelines: Art & design
Using materials, techniques, skills and media:
Using media; Using visual elements
Expressing feelings, ideas, thoughts and solutions:
Creating and designing; Communicating.

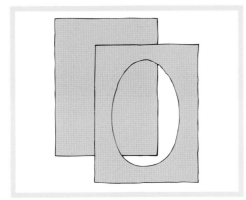

Step 2

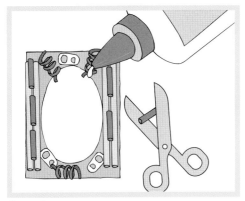

Step 3

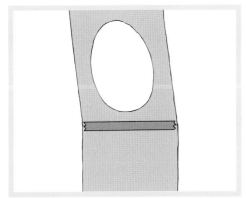

Step 4

Steps to follow

1 Each child will need two pieces of cardboard of the same size.

2 Cut a square, circle or free-form shape from the centre of one piece of cardboard to make the frame.

3 Glue the 'found objects' to the frame. Glue the larger pieces first. Be aware of the design that is developing. Vary lengths, colours and sizes of objects.

4 When the glue is dry, place the frame over the other piece of cardboard. Make sure that the edges are even. Flip the top piece up and connect the two frame parts with masking tape (on the inside) to form a hinge.

5 Insert a favourite piece of artwork or a photo and tape it in place.

Design principles to consider

● Repetition of shapes, lines, or colours
Repeating shapes in a design can lend continuity.

● Variation of sizes and shapes
Using large and small objects adds interest to a design.

● Contrasting colours in a pattern
Use of contrasting colours creates a design that is easier to see.

Paper quilts

Age range: 5–11 years

Create a quilt design using wallpaper remnants.

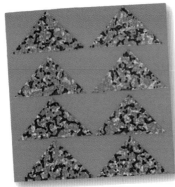

Vocabulary

contrast   design

patterning   symmetrical

Materials

• wallpaper remnants

• scissors

• glue stick

• 15 cm square coloured card

• ruler

• pencil

Project notes

• Weaving is mainly repetition and patterning. It involves organization of colour and texture into a pleasing design. Although quilting is not thought of as weaving, the repetition of colour and design is valuable when learning about pattern. It helps to talk first about patterning and the repetition of colour and shape when working on this project. Show quilt patterns to the children, then show a weaving such as a rug that has a definite pattern.

Let's talk about it

• Can you see how a weaver uses colour, shape and repetition to create the desired pattern in weaving?

• Why is it easier to design with paper first instead of designing directly on the loom?

National Curriculum: Art & design
KS1: 2a, 2b, 4a, 4b, 5b, 5c
KS2: 2a, 2b, 2c, 4a, 4b, 5b, 5c
QCA Schemes of Work: Art & design
Unit 1B – Investigating materials
Unit 3B – Investigating pattern
Scottish 5–14 Guidelines: Art & design
Using materials, techniques, skills and media:
Using media; Using visual elements
Expressing feelings, ideas, thoughts and solutions:
Creating and designing; Communicating

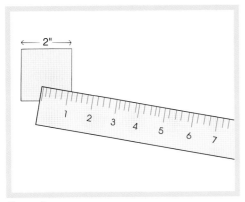

Step 1

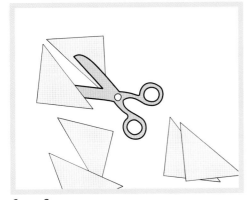

Step 2

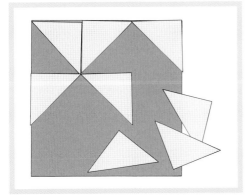

Step 3

Steps to follow

1 Choose a wallpaper remnant for colour and contrast. Using a ruler and pencil, measure and cut the remnant into 5 cm squares.

2 Cut the squares diagonally to form triangles and then cut those diagonally again.

3 Place the triangles on the coloured card and arrange them in a pleasing design. Be aware of repeating shapes when planning.

4 Glue the triangles in place.

Typical quilt patterns

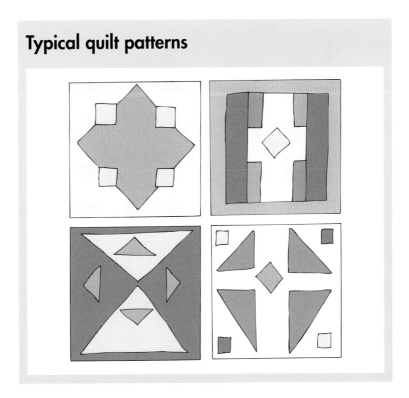

Japanese dolls

Age range: 7–11 years

Create a Japanese doll from reusable paper items while learning paper-folding techniques.

Vocabulary

kimono   obi

origami

Materials

- paper towel tube
- white glue or hot glue
- 15 x 18 cm white tissue paper (head)
- 15 x 5 cm blue tissue paper (hair)
- wrapping paper in assorted colours:
  - first neckband – 5 x 15 cm
  - second neckband – 10 x 20 cm
  - underdress – 15 x 18 cm
  - outer kimono – 25.5 x 18 cm
  - obi – 5 x 15 cm
- cotton wool balls
- craft stick
- stapler
- two ball-top straight pins (optional)
- red and black fine-point felt pens

Project notes

- Ask the children to collect paper tubes and used wrapping paper ahead of time.
- If papers are wrinkled, iron them on a low setting or press them between books.

Let's talk about it

- Why is paper folding important in this project?
- Why is it important to follow each step when creating a craft project?
- How is the texture of the face and hair different from the kimono?

National Curriculum: Art & design
KS1: 2a, 2b, 4a, 4b, 4c, 5b, 5c
KS2: 2a, 2b, 2c, 4a, 4b, 4c, 5b, 5c

QCA Schemes of Work: Art & design
Unit 1B – Investigating materials
Unit 5C – Talking textiles
Unit 6B – What a performance

Scottish 5–14 Guidelines: Art & design
Using materials, techniques, skills and media:
Using media; Using visual elements
Expressing feelings, ideas, thoughts and solutions:
Creating and designing; Communicating

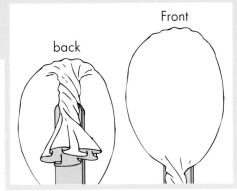

Step 1

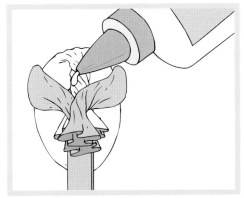

Step 2

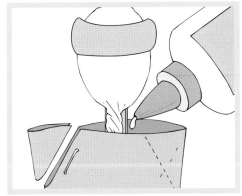

Step 3

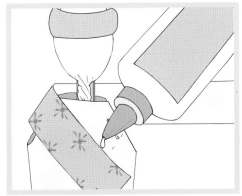

Step 4

Steps to follow

1 Make the head. Lay the white tissue on a clean surface and place one or two cotton wool balls in the centre. Fold the paper lengthwise over the cotton wool balls and twist the ends together tightly. Glue the head to one end of the craft stick, keeping the twisted ends facing down. Draw eyes and a mouth with felt pens.

2 Make the hair. Place one cotton wool ball in the centre of the tissue. Pull the cotton wool ball a little for a slightly longer shape, then roll it in the tissue. Wrap the roll around the top of the head. Twist the ends in the back and glue in place.

3 Place the craft stick with the head attached into the top of the paper tube and glue it in place. Staple the top of the tube closed on either side of the stick. Snip the corners of the tube at an angle for shoulders.

4 Make the neckbands. Fold the first neckband in half lengthwise. Lay the neck of the tube on the centre of this paper. Fold the paper to the front like a scarf and glue in place. Repeat this process with the second neckband, laying it slightly below the first neckband. (See picture on next page, step 5.)

Japanese dolls

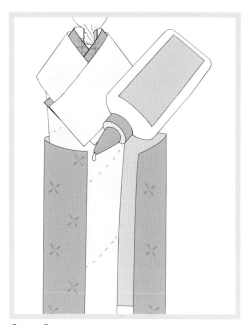

Step 5

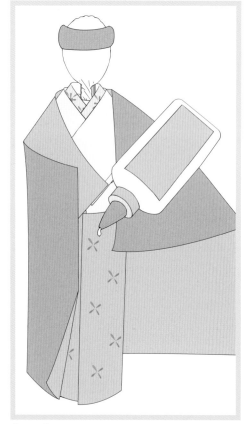

Step 6

Steps to follow

5 Make the underdress. Wrap the bottom half of the tube with the underdress paper. Glue it in place.

6 Make the outer kimono. Fold down 3 cm along the long edge of the outer kimono paper. Place the neck portion of the tube on the top centre of the kimono and fold over like a scarf. Glue it in place. Take the outer corners of the paper kimono and fold to the centre to make sleeves. Glue them in place. The arms will look folded.

7 Make the obi (sash). Fold the wrapping paper in quarters lengthwise. Wrap it around the hip area, securing with glue. Add a bow if you wish.

8 You may add a fan to the back of the head. Accordion-fold some paper and glue the ends together. Then glue the fan to the back of the head. Add two ball-top pins in the hair for decoration.

Making dolls has been a serious art form in Japan since the seventeenth century. Many dolls are made of plaster, rice paper or silk.

Nature

Nature is all around us and has always been a great creative inspiration for arts and crafts in many different cultures. Flowers, trees, rocks, animals, weather and a wide range of landscapes all have their own colours, forms, lines, patterns, shapes and textures that can be incorporated into art and crafts.

This chapter looks at craft projects that combine objects of nature with other materials to make cards, paper, mats, candles, model mice, sun catchers and model sheep.

The natural materials used in the projects can be easily recognised and collected by children. They include flowers, sand, shells, acorns and wool.

Through these craft projects, children can develop the skills to explore and investigate how natural objects can be used in art. By practising the basic craft ideas shown in this chapter, children will gain the confidence to see their ideas through to fruition.

Contents

Handmade paper

Age range: 7–11 years

Create handmade papers containing dried flowers and leaves while learning the art of papermaking

Vocabulary

deckle

paper

mould

fibre

Materials

- scraps of recyclable paper
- small flowers and leaves (dried and pressed)
- scissors
- a mould and deckle (see instructions on page 111)
- absorbent fabric (such as felt or a blanket)
- large bowl or sink
- blender
- water
- sponge

Project notes

- Some papers will be thin and some will be thick depending on the type of paper being used.
- You may trim the paper sheets to create straight edges or leave them as they come off the mould with ragged edges.

Let's talk about it

- How is the texture of handmade paper different from machine-made paper?
- What kinds of natural fibres can be used in making paper?

National Curriculum: Art & design
KS1: 2a, 2b, 4a, 4b, 5b, 5c
KS2: 2a, 2b, 2c, 4a, 4b, 5b, 5c
QCA Schemes of Work: Art & design
Unit 1B – Investigating materials
Unit 2B – Mother Nature, designer
Scottish 5–14 Guidelines: Art & design
Using materials, techniques, skills and media:
Using media; Using visual elements
Expressing feelings, ideas, thoughts and solutions:
Creating and designing; Communicating

Step 2

Step 3

Step 4

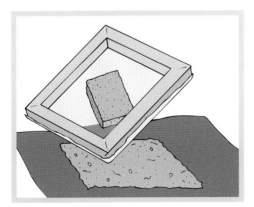

Step 6

Steps to follow

1 Cut and tear small pieces of paper and soak in water to soften.

2 Place approximately 60 ml of paper in the blender and fill with water. (You may also add small leaves and flower bits as long as the paper content exceeds the amount of plant matter.)

3 Fill the bowl or sink with water. Pour the blended mixture into the water until you have a thin layer of fibre floating on the top of the water. Add the pressed leaves and flowers to this mixture. You may even add glitter to liven up the texture.

4 Place the mould on top of the deckle screen. Hold them firmly together. Dip into the bowl and scoop up a layer of the mixture onto the screen.

5 Transfer the sheet of fibre to a damp piece of absorbent fabric by removing the mould and placing the deckle on the fabric with the paper side down.

6 Press repeatedly on the back of the deckle with a sponge to release the paper. Gently lift the deckle, leaving the paper on the fabric. Let the paper dry for 24 hours.

How to make a mould and deckle

Materials
• two small frames the same size

• screening with small holes

• thumbtacks

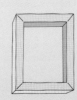

mould
(a frame)

deckle
(a frame, the same size as the mould, with fibreglass, plastic or wire screen)

Raffia mats

Age range: 5–11 years

Use basic weaving skills to create a small mat from natural raffia.

Vocabulary

braiding

raffia

warp

weft

Materials

- raffia
- cardboard
- scissors
- pencil and straight edge
- tape
- glue
- a plate (approximately 13 cm diameter)

Project notes

- Raffia can be found at most art supply stores and in school supply catalogues. Raffia does not have to be cut. It can be used in the random lengths in which it comes.

Let's talk about it

- What kinds of natural materials are used in weavings?
- What other useful objects could be woven from raffia?
- How is the texture of raffia different from other weaving materials?

National Curriculum: Art & design
KS1: 2a, 2b, 4a, 4b, 5b, 5c
KS2: 2a, 2b, 2c, 4a, 4b, 5b, 5c
QCA Schemes of Work: Art & design
Unit 1B – Investigating materials
Unit 2B – Mother Nature, designer
Scottish 5–14 Guidelines: Art & design
Using materials, techniques, skills and media:
Using media; Using visual elements
Expressing feelings, ideas, thoughts and solutions:
Creating and designing

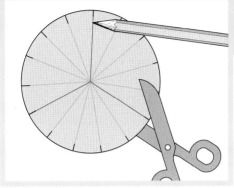

Step 1

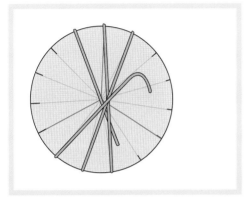

Step 2

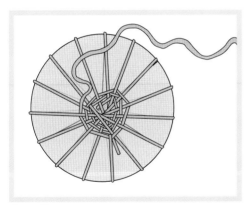

Step 3

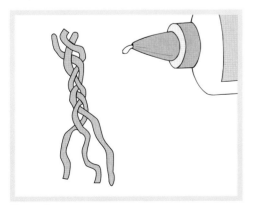

Step 5

Steps to follow

1 Make the cardboard weaving frame by tracing around a plate. Using a pencil, divide the frame into thirds. Then divide each third into 5 parts. Now there will be 15 sections. An adult will need to do this for younger children. Make a small notch at the edge of each line to hold the warp strands.

2 Create the warp. Fasten one end of a raffia strand to the frame with tape. Begin creating the warp by winding the raffia from each notch to the opposite notch, working around the frame until all notches have been used. The end of the raffia strand may be taped to keep it in place.

3 Begin weaving the weft. Using a separate strand of raffia, begin weaving in and out of the warp strands. Work from the centre towards the outer edge. Keep the weft close so the weaving will not have holes or gaps. When the weaving is finished, tie off the weft strand to make it secure.

4 Weave the other side of the frame in the same manner.

5 Make a decorative border around the mat by braiding a piece of raffia and securing it to the edge with glue (see page 27).

Sand candles

Create a free form candle using wax and sand.

Vocabulary

free form

paraffin

wick

Materials

- sand
- wax (paraffin)
- wick or string
- thermometer
- double boiler
- deep pan or tub
- heat source
- water
- broken crayons (with paper removed)
- toothpicks

Project notes

- Always use caution when working with hot wax. Never melt wax directly on a heat source; always use a double boiler. An adult must pour the wax.

- Old crayons are used to add colour to the wax.

Let's talk about it

- Why are these candles considered free form?

- What natural resources were used in making this candle?

- How is the texture of the sand different from the texture of the wax?

- Why was sand necessary to create this candle?

National Curriculum: Art & design
KS1: 2a, 2b, 4a, 4b, 5b, 5c
KS2: 2a, 2b, 2c, 4a, 4b, 5b, 5c
QCA Schemes of Work: Art & design
Unit 1B – Investigating materials
Scottish 5–14 Guidelines: Art & design
Using materials, techniques, skills and media:
Using media; Using visual elements
Expressing feelings, ideas, thoughts and solutions:
Creating and designing; Communicating

Step 2

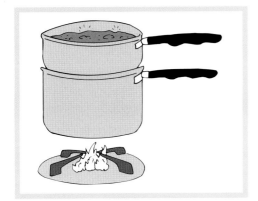

Step 3

Step 4

Steps to follow

1 Begin by putting sand into a tub or deep pan. Add enough water to make the sand damp (not wet).

2 Break pieces of wax into the melting pot. Add the thermometer and heat the wax to 80° Celsius.

3 While the wax is melting, create a mould in the sand. Ask younger children to press one of their hands into the sand to make an impression at least 1.25 cm deep. Older children may want to create an interesting shape or irregular design in the sand. Place a toothpick standing straight up in the centre of each sand mould. This will be used later to place the wick.

4 When the wax has melted, add broken pieces of crayon. This will add colour to the candle. When the crayons have melted, pour the wax into the forms pressed in the sand. (This must be done by an adult.) Let the wax set until it is hard (approximately one hour).

5 Dig gently under the candle and lift it out of the sand. Leave as much sand stuck to the wax as possible.

6 Remove the toothpick and insert a wick. Tie a knot in the end of the wick on the underside of the candle or secure it with a metal stopper.

Shell flowers

Age range: 5–11 years

Create flowers using shells from nature and basic art materials.

Vocabulary

form

shape

texture

Materials

- shells
- wire coat hangers
- wire cutters
- 8 cm strips of green tissue paper
- green card
- scissors
- glue gun and hot glue
- white glue

Project notes

- Establish safety rules for use of the glue gun. With younger children, an adult should do this step.
- These flowers make wonderful Mother's Day gifts.

Let's talk about it

- What kinds of textures do you see and feel with your shell flower?
- How does the form and shape of the shell resemble a flower?
- What other natural objects could be used to make flowers?

National Curriculum: Art & design
KS1: 1a, 2a, 2b, 4a, 4b, 5b, 5c
KS2: 1a, 2a, 2b, 2c, 4a, 4b, 5b, 5c

QCA Schemes of Work: Art & design
Unit 1B – Investigating materials
Unit 2B – Mother Nature, designer

Scottish 5–14 Guidelines: Art & design
Using materials, techniques, skills and media:
Investigating visually and recording; Using media;
Using visual elements
Expressing feelings, ideas, thoughts and solutions:
Creating and designing; Communicating

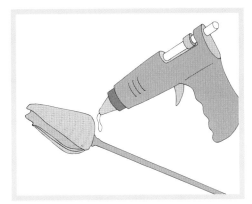
Step 2

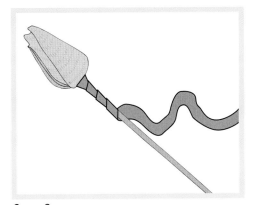
Step 3

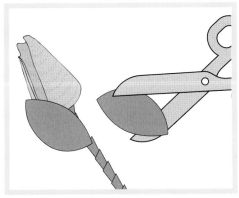
Step 4

Steps to follow

1 Collect shells of various shapes. Wash them. If there is no access to a beach where shells can be collected, purchase them from a craft store. Talk about the different shapes and forms and what flowers they resemble.

2 Cut the wire hangers to make the stems. Start the flower by hot-glueing a length of wire to the base of the shell. Let the glue dry thoroughly.

3 Take a strip of green tissue paper. Add a small amount of white glue to the base of the shell flower to hold the tissue in place. Wrap the tissue tightly around the wire. Overlap it a bit as you continue down the length of the stem. Dot some white glue on the wire stem while wrapping to hold the tissue in place.

4 Cut leaves from green card or the green tissue. Glue the leaves to the finished stem.

5 If you have enough materials, let the children make several flowers, and arrange them in a bouquet.

Acorn mice

Vocabulary

craft

Materials

- acorns (for the heads)
- walnut half shells (for the beds)
- white glue
- 5 cm fabric squares (for the blankets)
- cotton wool balls (for the bodies)
- 10 cm lengths of wool (for the tails)
- 15 cm lengths of wool (for the hangers)
- grey or brown felt (for the ears)
- black felt-tip marker

Project notes

- Explain how important it is to follow directions when doing craft projects.
- Talk about how things from nature can be formed into art. If you live in an area where it is possible, take a nature walk to collect the nuts.

Let's talk about it

- Why are crafts important?
- Do you see how some things from nature can be made to resemble other things from nature?
- How are the colour and texture of the acorns and walnuts alike? How are they different?

National Curriculum: Art & design
KS1: 2a, 2b, 4a, 4b, 5b, 5c
KS2: 2a, 2b, 2c, 4a, 4b, 5b, 5c
QCA Schemes of Work: Art & design
Unit 1B – Investigating materials
Unit 2B – Mother Nature, designer
Unit 5C – Talking textiles
Scottish 5–14 Guidelines: Art & design
Using materials, techniques, skills and media:
Investigating visually and recording; Using media;
Using visual elements
Expressing feelings, ideas, thoughts and solutions:
Creating and designing.

Steps 2 and 3

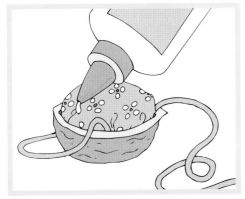

Step 4

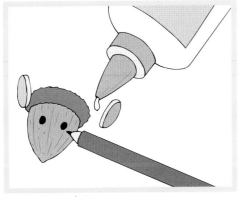

Steps 5 and 6

Step 7

Steps to follow

1 Collect acorns that still have their caps. The cap looks like a hat for the mouse. If the cap has fallen off, glue it back on with white glue.

2 Fold the longer piece of wool in half and glue it to the inside of the round sides of the walnut shell. This will be the loop for hanging the mouse.

3 Glue the smaller piece of wool to the inside of the pointed end of the walnut shell. This will be the tail.

4 Cover a cotton wool ball (or two) with fabric and glue it/them to the inside of the walnut shell. Make sure that all the cotton is covered and that the fabric ends are glued down. This is the body of the mouse wrapped in a blanket.

5 Use a felt-tip pen to draw eyes on the mouse's face.

6 Glue pieces of felt to the head for ears.

7 Glue the head to the covered cotton at the end of the shell opposite the tail.

Sun catchers

Create a sun catcher using dried flowers and wax.

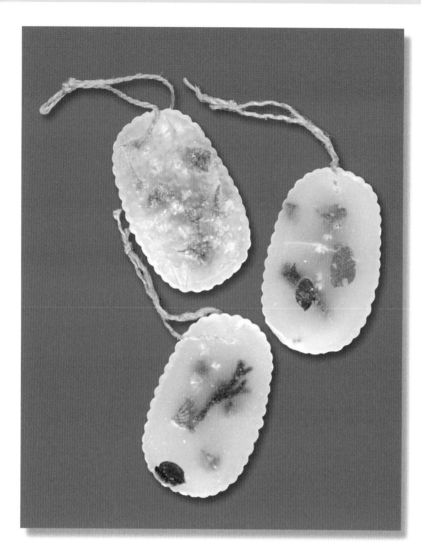

Vocabulary

colour

hue

paraffin

transparent

Materials

- paraffin (wax)
- double boiler
- string
- dried flowers
- moulds (such as small tart pans)
- toothpicks
- spray cooking oil

Project notes

- Use caution when melting wax.
  - Never melt wax directly over the heat source.
  - Always use a double boiler.
  - An adult must pour the wax.
- If you do not have moulds, you can use any small, shallow can.

Let's talk about it

- What colours are best for this project?
- How does the transparency of the wax help this project work?
- What will happen if something made with wax gets too hot?

National Curriculum: Art & design
KS1: 2a, 2b, 4a, 4b, 5b, 5c
KS2: 2a, 2b, 2c, 4a, 4b, 5b, 5c
QCA Schemes of Work: Art & design
Unit 1B – Investigating materials
Unit 2B – Mother Nature, designer
Scottish 5–14 Guidelines: Art & design
Using materials, techniques, skills and media:
Using media; Using visual elements
Expressing feelings, ideas, thoughts and solutions:
Creating and designing

Step 3

Step 4

Step 5

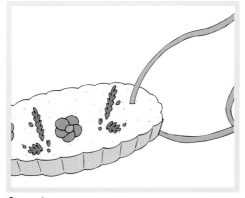

Step 6

Steps to follow

1 Collect small flowers and leaves. Set them aside to dry for several days.

2 Spray the moulds with cooking oil to prevent the wax from sticking to them.

3 Melt the wax in a double boiler. When the wax has melted, pour it into the moulds to a thickness of about 0.5 cm.

4 Drop dried flowers and leaves into the wax in the mould.

5 When the wax starts to harden, place a toothpick 0.5 cm from the top to make a hole for the string.

6 After the wax is completely solid, remove the shape from the mould. Remove the toothpick. Thread a string through the hole. Hang the sun catcher in a shaded window. (Direct sunlight will melt the wax.)

Dried flower cards

Create beautiful stationery from dried and pressed flowers.

Vocabulary

arrangement

colour

design

Materials

- dried flowers and leaves
- 15 x 23 cm art paper
- white glue
- books for pressing
- spray fixative (optional)

Project notes

- Collect flowers when they are in season and press them for this project. Children enjoy seeing how different flowers look after they are pressed.

- Talk about design principles when planning these cards: repetition of shapes, variation of sizes and contrasting colours.

Let's talk about it

- What textures and colours can you find in nature?
- How were the dried/pressed flowers different from fresh-picked flowers?
- Why are colours and textures important in this project?

National Curriculum: Art & design
KS1: 1a, 2a, 2b, 4a, 4b, 5b, 5c
KS2: 1a, 2a, 2b, 2c, 4a, 4b, 5b, 5c
QCA Schemes of Work: Art & design
Unit 1B – Investigating materials
Unit 2B – Mother Nature, designer
Scottish 5–14 Guidelines: Art & design
Using materials, techniques, skills and media:
Investigating visually and recording; Using media;
Using visual elements
Expressing feelings, ideas, thoughts and solutions:
Creating and designing

Step 1

Step 4

Steps to follow

1 Press fresh flowers and leaves. Put them between blotting papers or paper towels. Place them in a book or between heavy weights. Check periodically to make sure the moisture is being absorbed.

2 Fold the art paper in half to create a card.

3 Choose pressed and dried flowers, leaves or seeds. Think about colour and texture as the design is arranged.

4 Start glueing the leaves or darker coloured flowers to the paper with white glue. Proceed by building up layers of flowers and leaves into a pleasing arrangement.

5 Let the card sit until all the glue is dry.

6 You may spray the card gently with a light fixative. An adult should do this in a well-ventilated area.

Woolly sheep

Use homespun or manufactured wool to create woolly sheep.

Vocabulary

fibre

weaving

Materials

- wool of any colour
- cardboard
- scraps of black card
- sheep pattern on page 125
- scissors
- black tempera paint
- glue

Project notes

- Use wool that children have spun to make this lesson even more rewarding.

Let's talk about it

- Where does wool come from?
- What other natural fibres can be woven?
- What fibres are manmade?

National Curriculum: Art & design
KS1: 1a, 2a, 2b, 4a, 4b, 5b, 5c
KS2: 1a, 2a, 2b, 2c, 4a, 4b, 5b, 5c

QCA Schemes of Work: Art & design
Unit 1B – Investigating materials
Unit 2B – Mother Nature, designer
Unit 5C – Talking textiles

Scottish 5–14 Guidelines: Art & design
Using materials, techniques, skills and media:
Investigating visually and recording; Using media;
Using visual elements
Expressing feelings, ideas, thoughts and solutions:
Creating and designing; Communicating

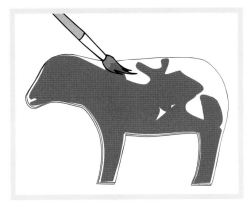

Step 2

Steps 3 and 4

Steps to follow

1 Trace the sheep pattern onto the cardboard. Cut it out.

2 Paint both sides of the sheep with the black paint. Let it dry thoroughly.

3 Wrap the wool around the body of the sheep, starting with the forehead and working back. Reverse direction after the shoulder. Tie a knot when the wrapping is complete.

4 Cut ears from black card. Glue the ears to the sheep.

Sheep and ear patterns

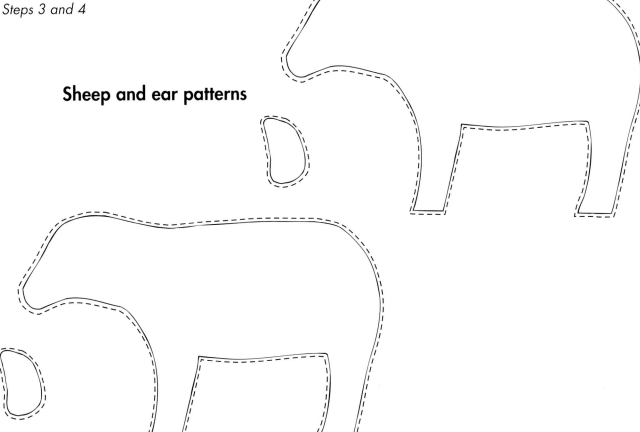

Glossary

abstract: a design that does not project any recognisable person or thing

arrangement: items placed in a specific order or design

add-on method: a method used when working with clay that involves adding new pieces of clay by attaching them with slip

background: the part of a picture behind the main object or objects

bookbinding: the cover that holds together pages of a book; the act of covering and binding a book

braiding: the act of interweaving three or more strands to create a plait or woven unit such as rope

camouflage: the art of concealment; to disguise things in their surroundings

candlewick: the string part of a candle

carving: the act of cutting wood, stone or other material to form a figure or design

clay: mud-like substance with good elasticity

collage: an artistic composition of materials and objects glued over a surface

colour: the pigment of an object

colour scheme: a combination of colours according to a general plan

complementary colours: colours directly opposite each other on the colour wheel (red and green, violet and yellow, blue and orange)

contrast: a striking difference, for example in the use of colours

cool colours: colours that give a calming feeling (blues, greens and purples)

craft: skill or ability in artwork done with the hands; to make by hand

Cubism: an art style characterised by geometric shapes

deckle: the part of equipment used in making paper that has the screen to catch the fibres

design: to prepare a plan for artwork; the overall effect of a piece of artwork

fantasy: an image not of the real worldd

fibre: plant, animal or man-made tissue or material

firing: the process of 'baking' clay objects at a very high heat in a special oven called a kiln

fixative: a spray solution applied to pieces of art to prevent smearing

folk art: traditional art of rural people

foreground: the part of a picture nearest the spectator

form: the design, structure or pattern of a work of art

free form: a shape or artwork created without mechanical aids or guidelines

geometric: use of simple shapes formed from straight or curved lines

geometric design: a plan for a painting that uses shapes

glaze: a liquid, glass-like paint used to seal and decorate pottery

hue: the gradation of a particular colour

impasto: a paint and paste mixture used to create texture in a painting

impression: an effect produced on the mind; an imprint, for example in clay

kiln: a type of oven that bakes clay at extremely high temperatures

kimono: a long-sleeved loose robe traditionally worn by the Japanese

landscape: a picture representing natural scenery

limited palette: a palette of two or three paints

loom: a device on which cloth is produced by interweaving thread or wool at right angles

medium: the substance used to create a painting or print

mixed media: more than one medium used together on one piece of artwork

mould: a form into which wax can be poured; the part of equipment used in making paper that determines the edges

monochromatic: having only one colour

monoprint: an impression made from one source onto a surface

name chop: a carved block used in printing a signature or design

negative space: the space surrounding a recognisable shape

obi: a wide sash worn with a kimono

optical illusion: a false appearance or impression

origami: the Japanese art of paper folding

paddling: a technique used in making pottery, in which a person slaps the object gently with a paddle (or similar object) to erase fingerprints and smooth lumps

painting: the act of representing objects on a surface using paint

paper: a material produced from wood pulp

papier-mâché: a material made from paper shreds mixed with glue that can be moulded when wet and becomes hard when dry

paraffin: a waxy, colourless mixture used to make candles

patterning: a design made of repeated markings

pigment: a substance used for colouring

pinching: a method used when working with clay by pinching the clay between the fingers to form a shape

positive space: a recognisable shape

primary colours: colours on the colour wheel that cannot be made by mixing other colours (red, blue and yellow)

priming: to prepare paints by adding water to soften them

printing: the act of stamping an impression onto a surface

pulling/ pull-out method: a method used to form a shape in clay that involves stretching the clay as opposed to adding on pieces of clay

raffia: a fibre from palm leaves used for weaving baskets and mats

realistic: an image found in the real world

reef knot: a common double knot that can be achieved by tying two loose ends first right over left, then left over right

relief print: a print made from a projection on a form

scoring: to make lines, cuts or notches on a surface to allow for better adherence when used with slip

sculpture: the art of shaping a three-dimensional design by carving and/or moulding

secondary colours: colours on the colour wheel that are made from two other colours (orange, green and purple)

shape: a definite form

shuttle: a device used in weaving to carry the weft threads back and forth through the warp

slip: a watery mixture of clay and water used in adhering pieces of clay together; also used in moulds to cast ceramic pieces

stencil: a thin sheet with a cut pattern so that applied paint or pastel can penetrate to another surface

still life: a picture consisting of inanimate objects

symmetry/ symmetrical: arrangement or balancing of objects; when two sides are exactly the same

technique: working method of performing a particular task

texture: the structure, feel and physical appearance of a piece of artwork due to the medium used

three-dimensional: having depth, height, and width

tin smithing: the art of making a design with light metals such as tin

transparent: capable of transmitting light

warm colours: colours that give the feeling of warmth (reds, oranges and yellows)

warp: the threads that run vertically in a weaving or on a loom

weaving: the act of interweaving fibres at right angles to create a fabric

weft: the threads that run horizontally in a weaving or on a loom

wet on wet technique: a painting technique where the paper is first wet with water, allowing the paint to blend when applied

wick: a cord of fibres that draws fuel to the flame as in candles